The Wonders of Winter

An anthology of poetry

celebrating the wonders

of the winter season

Timothy Couchman

Selection Editor

Paul Gilliland

Editor-in-Chief

Southern Arizona Press

Southern Arizona Press

Southern
Arizona
Press

The mission of Southern Arizona Press is to promote the works of self-published and lesser-known unpublished authors and poets to the rest of the world through publishing themed and unthemed anthologies and assisting in the publication and promotion of their works.

It is our desire to make the voices of these aspiring poets and authors available to as wide an audience as possible with the belief that no writer of poetry or literature should ever have to pay to have their works published.

The Wonders of Winter

If you would like your work to be considered for future anthologies, please visit us at
http://www.southernarizonapress.com/current-submissions/
for a full list of current open anthology submissions and submission guidelines.

Published by Southern Arizona Press
Sierra Vista, Arizona 85635
www.southernarizonapress.com

Follow us on Facebook at:
https://www.facebook.com/SouthernArizonaPress

Selection Editor – Timothy Couchman
Format, cover design, and edits by Paul Gilliland, Editor-in-Chief, Southern Arizona Press

Poets photos Copyright © retained by submitting poets

ISBN: 9781960038012

Table of Contents

Eileen Sateriale is a freelance writer living in Massachusetts. She retired from the Federal Government after working for many years as an analyst. Her poetry has appeared in the Southern Arizona Press Anthology *The Stars and the Moon in the Evening Sky*; Capsule Stories; Peeking Cat Anthology; Poets are Heroes Magazine; Mused Literary Review; Blue Heron Review: *The BeZine Sustainability and Ukraine Peace Special Edition*; Postcards, Poems and Prose Magazine; and Flora Fiction. She has had short stories published in Let Us Not Forget anthology, Forget Me Knots anthology, and Flora Fiction website. Many years ago, she was publicity liaison for her daughters' school and for one year, wrote a column for the Prince George's *Sentinel* as well as contributing to the *Washington Post*. She has had travel articles accepted on *We Said Go Travel* as well as three non-fiction pieces in the *Online Biographical Dictionary of the Woman Suffrage Movement in the United States* to commemorate the 100th anniversary of the passage of the nineteenth amendment.

She can be contacted at ewsateriale@verizon.net

Aurora Borealis

Pale green light in sky
blushed by tints of pink and blue
and rare violet hues
spindly pine trees tickle heaven.

Previously published in *Postcards, Poems, and Prose Magazine*

Harbinger of Winter

An early dusk
frigid breezes
bare branches

shrill shriek
big black crow
early dark sky

dead autumn leaves
cling to tree branches
by relentless wind

empty caw
signals a harbinger
of winter.

Fire In the Family Room

Put three dry logs in the fireplace.
Peek up the chimney and open the flue
Add crumbled up newspaper and kindling.
Light a match and hope it catches.

If the match doesn't, light another.
Is the fire catching?
Yes, it is! It's a roaring fire!
Take the fireplace poker and rearrange the logs.

Crackle, crackle, pop, snap.
The sounds of an intriguing fire.
The orange and yellow flames a foot and a half tall
Wavering in the breeze from the flue.

Let's cook some popcorn for the youngsters.
Stray kernels scatter to the floor.
The ten year old shoves popcorn in her mouth.
And says, "Look at the logs getting smaller."

The ends of logs are starting to burn up.
The twelve-year-old puts on another log.
Boom! Another log added to the fire.
It catches on the existing sparks! Just like magic!

Time for the kids to go to bed.
Let's snuggle near the fire while the heat warms the
    room.
Hold hands with me. I don't care about the T.V.
The fire is much more interesting!

Montreal Express

From the north comes the Montreal Express
that makes cold lovers bundle to excess.
Canada's blasting breeze
makes us cough and wheeze.
Into the house, we jockey
to watch a game of hockey
and escape the paralyzing brisk mess.

An Icy Night in the City

Skinny, bone like trees
that have lost their leaf cover
stand naked in the dark of nightfall.
Their finger-like arthritic branches
create an uneven archway
over a carved out snow-covered dirt path.
Dusk falls on the landscape.
Factories create a sooty air
that grays the atmosphere.
The temperature has fallen;
the snow crusted to ice.
Rubble litters the streets.
Worn out child's toys accidently
dropped on the sidewalk
invoke a hazardous eyesore.
Guided by the blurry street lamps,
travelers dressed in layers and warm caps
trudge through the snow,
watching their feet and looking ahead.
The dirty air stings their lungs
and hurts their eyes.
Commuters must watch carefully
where they step for ice and litter
can be treacherous and
urban beauty can be
quickly destroyed.

Alaska Wilderness

Bright sun
low in the sky
allows wild game to seek
shelter from hungry men who want
their meat.

Snow moon
illuminates
dark, bleak December sky
letting weary, frozen hunters
trudge home.

Foreshadowing

A few months ago,
the sun danced what
seemed like forever
emitting warmth and
bright light.
Now, late afternoon,
the sky dark turns gray
foreshadowing an
ominous time of year.
When the days get cold
The distant beaver moon
provides no comfort
in this darkest hour.

Rhiannon Owens moved to Merthyr Tydfil from the North-West of England after bagging herself a handsome Welsh boy, Nicholas. She loves her cat, her mid-life crisis dresses, reading, and making her messy garden look even worse. As well as working on solo writing projects Rhiannon has had six poetry books published along with her writing partner, the super talented Ashley O'Keefe.

Ashley O'Keefe is a son, brother, husband, father, and uncle from Merthyr Tydfil, South Wales. 2020 saw him complete his first feature film screenplay and have two poetry book collaborations published with the incredibly talented Rhiannon Owens, 2021 has seen them publish two additional books with a fifth again in 2022. 2022 has also seen the two writing partners publish their first themed poetry book called *Nocturnals*.

Their books are available on Amazon.

The link to their poetry page:

https://www.facebook.com/RhiannoAsleyPoetry/

Rhiannon has had poems featured in three previous Southern Arizona Press anthologies and we are delighted to have six of her poems plus one of her collaborations with Ashley O'Keefe included in this anthology.

Eiderdown

Fireflowers explode in the sky
Green, purple, magenta,
Orange sparks in our shining eyes,
And leaves of confetti
Kiss our faces and whisper in our ears
As they dance across the ground
And the delicious crunch underfoot reminds us that
Winter is near,
We bundle ourselves up cosy
And clasp gloved hands,
A colourful eiderdown of bronze, crimson, russet and
yellow
Stretches before us
As we dream of slipping between the sheets,
Warming each other with entwined limbs, passion
And body heat...

Beauty

One year the Winter did not end
The landscape was desolate and stark
No birdsong
No flowers
No blue in the sky
All was silent, all was dark,

Outside only Winter
As far as the eye could see,
Bare branches so gnarled
And so twisted,
In their naked vulnerability
The wind howled and bit
A bone numbing chill in the air
But it did not faze me,
I did not fret
I did not care…

Because I see only beauty
Such beauty everywhere!

In my smile
A morning sunrise,
Sunshine lighting up
My eyes

One year the Winter did not end
The landscape was desolate and stark
No birdsong
No flowers
No blue in the sky
All was silent, all was dark,

People shuffle on by
In misery
Faces downturned
Against blizzard and snow
But I slip and slide
Along the frosty paths
My laughter rings out
My frostbitten cheeks glow,

Because I see only beauty
Such beauty everywhere!

In my smile
A morning sunrise,
Sunshine lighting up
My eyes

The Winter does not end
The Summer is no longer here
But why should that cloud my heart
When I can feel you near!

Winter's Sight

Traversing this endless vista
our numb fingers intertwined,
trees are crystallized
shimmering with ethereal light

If only you could see...

but the sharp, cold air
slaps our faces
with hard blunt kisses,
feverish kisses that burn

and the smell of decay
and rebirth fills the air

Snow has powdered your eyelashes,
dusted them
as I long to dust them with kisses,
your white lips smile toward me
and I yearn to
kiss them rosy again

Tiny intricate snowflakes
settle on my hand,
too exquisite to be caught
as perfect as you,
fleeting shards of joy,
transient,
teasing,
infuriating

If only you could see

You catch them on your tongue
and your laughter is like pearls,
pearls of ice
smooth
and hard, and stinging

If only you could see
If only you would see me

A Winter Wander

Walk, breathe
and live in the moment,
in the here and now
with no worries on your mind
and nothing to make you frown,
get the blood circulating
enjoy the scenery,
enjoy nature's abundance
which remains undaunted
despite a picture that is wintry,
because red berries shine like rubies
and pine trees reach out a friendly bough,
you walk and everything
is serenity
in the frost-kissed here and now,
and when you return back home
to the bosom of your family,
you'll feel content and warm
just being with them,
surrounded by love
as the cat purrs away on your knee.

White Swans and Ice

Through frozen dreams I ride a white swan
as necks elegantly arch into feathered hearts,
the embrace of lovers as they become one

and the ice is not cold, I am not numb
I've come alive, sailing into this silvered night,
the sky is flawless onyx, smooth obsidian illuminated
by the purity of the moon and stars,

I have journeyed far
right through the crystalline curtain of ice
now hanging gossamer-like,

A fixed cascade of sparkling perfection
a backdrop to this place where all my dreams came
    true….

The Hunter's Moon Of Snow

The radiant Snow Moon of February
larger than life, a 'Storm Moon'
such luminosity in the light of it
light of this moon, au Clair de la Lune.

The 'Hunger Moon' it was known
to the American tribes of the North,
in the hard hunting conditions of mid-winter
with food scarce and hard to source.

They would stare up at this Moon
in the desolate, unforgiving terrain
but still give thanks, respecting Nature
despite frozen ground, and vast craggy plains.

Heads bowed this circle of elders
in spiritual ritual, each tribe's varied traditions
hope offered for sighting of buffalo
as the Snow Moon watches over all,
and she listens.

All over the World she has watched
and listened to many a prayer,
but for these noble, dauntless tribes
she feels a fierce, protective flare.

Snow Moon of mid-winter
luminous in the night sky
glowing Clair de Lune
'Hunter's Moon' way up high.

Winter's Past

Rivers meet and converge
Hearts seldom do the same,
Save when they've loved and lost
But then find their beloved again,

Like fairytales and fables
Sweet damsels in distress,
The chivalry that turns to more
As hands roam and undress...

Honoured to be loved
By someone brave and true,
A champion through the mists of time
Beloved I've found in you,

I met you in the winter
The river steely gray,
The wind biting through our skin
Bone-cold; yet still our hearts were gay...

Through all the storms and battles
With time not on our side,
We make the most of what we share
On to another quest we ride...

When the water ices over
Becomes a river of frozen glass,
A thaw is never far away
Hearts melting, Winter's past

In collaboration with Ashley O'Keefe.

Carol Edwards is a northern California native transplanted to southern Arizona. She lives and works in relative seclusion with her books, plants, and pets (+ husband). She grew up reading fantasy and classic literature, climbing trees, and acquiring frequent grass stains. She enjoys a coffee addiction and raising her succulent army. Her work has most recently appeared in anthologies from Southern Arizona Press, The Ravens Quoth Press, and White Stag Publishing, and is forthcoming in Space & Time issue #142.

Blanket

Icy cold cuts through my robe
thinned from so many years of use.

Bare feet freeze on flagstone
that just hours ago

held the remains of winter's heat –
naked to the slightest breeze,

they tremble at its kiss, at its ability
to kill – lured out by the pale

veil draped on the world,
the full moon's cure to ills,

pain split-second relieved as we
gaze the skies, moon ruled on one side,

chased daily by the relentless sun.
My skinny dog jumps into my lap

and huddles close; I wish I'd brought
a blanket to wrap us up in

while we sit silently shivering
to watch the light rise.

Southern Arizona Press

Mid-Winter Moonrise

Inspired by Icka M Chif's winter landscape photography

Mist-shrouded yellow eye
hangs on the horizon, baleful
gaze streams dim through trees,
barren branches scratches leave

on an anemic blushed sky,
sunset's blood diluted in air,
frozen like the ground that wears
moonlight captured in piled drifts,
woods and orchards lifeless.

Dead clinging leaves rattle and hiss
scrape their sides like dragon scales –
shadowless it rests its wings,
searing colder than the north wind gale
blankets Earth in glacial breath

clutches her throat in claws of death;
the very sun its jaws devour,
and darkness comes with every hour
to seep in walls and doors and souls,
herald of silvery silence, hard as stone,

frigid kiss of madness to bestow:
lightning passion's icy burn,
fate of all poor pilgrims whose hearts return
to beat and break 'neath a starry wilderness
robed in chatoyant opalescence.

Previously published on the poet's blog *Practically Poetical*
(practicallypoetical.wordpress.com)

Soft Lies

We dream
to soar on snow white wings
up an azure winter sky,
to rend through shale haze
dimming the pale sun –

    Such soft lies the clouds tell us.
    On high: a bed of down and fluff.
    Below: a dark storm brewing.

Revolve

The cold is lovely this evening,
Winter's last breath
before harsh summer descends,
the desert transformed
into an oven
baking plants to a crisp,
sidewalks and streets fried
until they sizzle all night;
even a dousing monsoon
merely makes them a sauna.

No, this coolness will only return
as Earth's tilt moves from the sun:
a reprieve

like lovers fighting,
or loving, pace
to the edges of a room,
gravity taut between them,
and take refuge in their favorite spaces,
for the moment granted peace
until they draw too close
and again re-heat.

Chiffon-thin hands
drift down from my window
to brush my arm, ankle,
her touch delicate,
young –
those fingers when next I feel them
will have aged,
skin tissue-paper thin
rasping on my cheek,
edges almost sharp enough
to cut.

Winter's fangs
lengthen in Autumn's mouth,
silent as snowdrifts piled all night;
whatever warmth she drains from me
cannot extend her life.

You Texted Me to Tell Me You're Thinking of Me So I Wrote You a Poem
For Lisa Walsh

It is a stormy day today,
the kind a gothic novel would approve:
sky gray and grumbling,
riotous hail dancing its short-lived steps,
bounces off everything it touches.

I imagine you, my friend, with your cup of tea,
standing at your window,
open slightly to freshen your house,
tease the flames in your hearth,

while the rain quenches thirsty mouths
agape in your garden,
that solitary sanctuary you go to read,
to meditate,
to simply be,
enjoy the life you're living,

though always there sits an open chair
in case you unexpectedly have company,
who, in your presence, savors a deep warmth,
like the cup in your hands
thaws your rock-climber fingers,

slowly waking in this last stretch of winter,
longing for spring days when they can
again grasp sun-drenched stones
where the wind plays its silly games
and open air calls your name.

But for now, I imagine you perfectly content,
the heat from your drink
whispering mist, a small performance to mirror
the greater billow surging by,

perhaps with piano music playing,
notes straying into room corners
as they trickle
from your speakers to the floor, roll
until they tickle your feet, then dart under the couch,

their little hands catching hold of the patter
droplets make, spin around in circles
like children on the playground
until you really can't separate them.

Patches of sunlight soon appear and disappear,
the world a little brighter,
as it always is to your eyes,
you who can see the beauty in everything,
even a few scribbled rhyming lines.

When a Winter Storm Sits on a Mountain

Avalanches of swollen
clouds surge, suspended,
shadows over bone-white peaks.

Diamond dust strains to stifle the sun,
glitters bright in its light.

Powder white waves crest in blue
while down rocky crags
murky fingers creep.

Frigid wind pulls strands of my hair
out from where I bound them,
tugs and dances at my shirt sleeves.

Winter tries to play
but no one really sees.

Previously published on the poet's blog *Practically Poetical*
(practicallypoetical.wordpress.com)

Pat Severin is a retired Christian school teacher living in Appleton, Wisconsin, where she has been writing and sharing her poetry for many years. She has been an active member of the Society of Children's Book Writers and Illustrators for the past four years. Her Christian poems have been published in four Christian Magazines, the *Agape* Review, the *Clayjar Review*, *The Way Back 2 Ourselves*, and *Pure in Heart Stories*. In addition to her poetry, she has written a heartfelt memoir of her mother's life.

Pat is thrilled to be featured in this, her fourth Southern Arizona Press Anthology. She is also one of the featured writers in the new book, *I Chose You, Perfectly Imperfect Rescue Dogs and their Humans* which is available on Amazon and *Chicken Soup for the Soul: Lessons Learned From My Dog*, which will be released January 24, 2023.

One of her most rewarding endeavors has been writing poems of encouragement for people going through difficult times and health struggles which she sends out weekly in her original cards.

Seasonal Reflections

As the days become shorter & cold breezes blow,
I'm reminded of autumns so long ago,
When taking for granted each color and nuance
I thoughtless pondered just what I would do once…
The piles were collected and I could jump in,
With playmates and neighbors. What a terrible din…
Of shouts, affirmations, "fall's finally here!"
How I loved my red nose and each freezing ear.

No hat, seldom coats, just a constant abandon,
Short days and long nights and putting my hand in…
Those gooey old pumpkins with wild, scary faces,
Combing closets and attics and various places…
To find just the perfect costume to wear,
Applying the make-up, Mom fixing my hair
To go door to door, was it trick or it treat?
All I knew was I'd soon have some goodies to eat!

Then stuffed to the gills I'd crawl into bed.
I knew, all too well, I'd been over fed!
And the days that soon followed how quickly they
    flew,
Thanksgiving vacation! I hadn't a clue…
What went into the turkey, the dressing and all,
And why they all called it the Great Butterball?
I may be much older and wiser today,
I'd much rather leave this old job and just play!
I know I was anxious a grownup to be,
But a jump in the leaves sounds MUCH better to me!

It's a Comin'

They say a storm's a comin.'
The forecast said, "Prepare!"
The snow's a fallin' rapidly
And there's no time to spare!

Make sure you turn the heat up
'Cause cold is seepin' in.
The winds are blowin' fierce, my dear,
Ya' hear that roarin' din?

Now, you had better bundle up,
Long underwear and boots,
Your scarf, your vest, your woolen hat,
Your snowmobile suit…

'Twill be your buffer from the cold,
For shov'lin' next in store!
Be sure to salt the walkway, too.
Come in and shut the door!

I'll put a pot of cocoa on;
Mmmm…chocolate fills the air!
I'll add some little marshmellows.
You've ice there in your hair.

Let's sit right near the fireplace
And watch the dancing flames.
Hey, we should ask the neighbors in
To play a couple games?

And when the neighbors all have left,
We'll both climb into bed
And snuggle 'neath the covers
Pulled way up to our heads.

We're warm at last, so how'd ya' feel?
"I guess that I'd say this:
We'd never feel this toasty warm
If not for winter's kiss."

They Were Too Few

Remember going sledding
Down that hill when you were young?
That whoosh of snow as you took off
When both your arms were swung?

Attempting to propel yourself
And give yourself some speed?
Remember what that feeling was
And how your soul felt freed?

Until you got the hang of it,
You thought the kids would laugh
If it was not a perfect ride,
So much faster than the last.

They noticed you had mastered it
And wanted to jump on.
You knew that you could handle it.
Conclusion was forgone…

That you were like the other kids,
Accepted that you had
Achieved the art of sledding now!
And you were awf'lly glad.

But worrying about that stuff,
It wasn't worth the bother.
In fact, sometimes you'd much prefer
Just going with your father.

But either way, that sledding
Was such fun, you couldn't wait…
To leave your bed and get your sled
And rush down through the gate…

And take right off to Wilson's Hill.
The snow had newly fallen!
Remember when you reached the top
The winter winds were callin'?

You'd rush to be the first one there
No other kids, just <u>you.</u>
Those days were memory-making days.
A shame they were too few.

Winter's Kiss

Now, there are some who can't abide
The winter cold, they'd sooner hide
Until the winds of summer come.
A little cold and they feel numb.

But when winds blow and children play
In snowsuits red and hats of grey,
It looks a wonderland to me
As snowflakes cling to yonder tree!

When all the world is draped in white,
I find it my complete delight.
The moon illuminates the sky
As critters romp and night birds fly.

'Twas not so long ago, I paused,
With sunburned face the sun had caused.
But summer can't compete with this.
'Tis nothing like the winter's kiss.

Unseasonable Warmth

Unseasonable warmth, what a wonderful phrase,
To again feel the temps of past Aprils and Mays.
Then just as we're in for a cold, arctic blast,
Comes this short interruption that we know will not last.
It reminds us of days that we hoped would just linger.
Although it's November, for last spring a dead ringer!
But we won't object and we cannot complain
Not even when sun is preempted by rain.
It's warm and we love it, though we know it's not right,
Just like turning the clock back to give us more light.
But it's foolish declaring it's wrong or it's right
When we all can enjoy every minute of light
Till the sun will not warm us or tan us with rays.
We'll just have to savor these unseasonable days
When the calendar tells us fall's over, it's winter,
And then for a moment our logic might splinter.
Though this temp makes no sense when it's almost December,
This warmth is a gift and one to remember
Because when harsh winds blow and snowstorms arrive,
We'll be longing for temps like this seventy-five!

Denis Murphy was born in 1959 in Cork, Ireland and now resides in Sligo, Ireland. He was a former Travel Consultant and Travel Agency Manager. A major turning point in his life came in 2007 when, at the age of 48, he was diagnosed with Parkinson's Disease. Anyone who suffers from this Disease, or has a family member who does, will know that it brings about drastic changes. It can be very difficult for people with Parkinson's to express their emotions, feelings and their loss of power and independence. All the more need for an outlet to express these emotions. He believes by sharing he can better understand what he is going through. One can get caught up in their own worries and forget that the disease not only affects their own lives, but also that of family, friends, and loved ones. They often feel as frustrated and confused as he does. He is very lucky to have such an understanding wife who has great patience, empathy, and understanding and provides her support, encouragement, inspiration, and love. The main themes of his poems are about coping with Parkinson's Disease, and his relationship with nature, life and with oneself. Poetry helps him appreciate this wonderful gift of life.

The Simplest Thing

It's a wet and windy, winter's day
Outside, the trees dance and sway
Like restless ghosts in the wind and rain
Raindrops rage against the window pane
Then slowly slide and trickle down 'til
They come to rest on the windowsill
The glowering light catches each drop
Like a string of diamonds, or a crystal teardrop
Sparkling like fireflies in old jam jars
A transparent curtain of twinkling stars

A Robin, alights on the old garden gates
Feathers all ruffled and patiently waits
Raindrops hang from the old rusty bars
Sparkling like diamonds or a thousand stars
There is so much beauty, to be found
If we just open our eyes and look around
Such peace and tranquility we can find
When we listen and still the restless mind
Look for the joy in the simplest thing
Enjoy the moment and hear your Heart sing.

A Cold Winter's Morning

On a cold winter's morning so pale and so bright
A canvas of muted colours in soft morning light
Images and outlines in shades of pastel
Imagined or real , difficult to tell
Half light and shadow deceive and play
Tricks on our senses, at this time of day
The winter sun, so faint and so pale
 Slanting sunlight peering through the thin veil
Tendrils of cloud like torn banners unfurled
Casting long shadows from another world
Like demented demons, dancing around
The sparkle of starlight on the glistening ground
As dew on the grass captures the sun's light
On a cold winter's morning, so pale and so bright.

The Song of the Wind Chime

A blanket of snow lay on the ground
A hushed silence for miles around
As if the world has forgotten to speak
Except for a chime so faint and so weak

A soft breath of wind catches an old wind chime
Caressing it gently, a memory of another time
Like a ripple of laughter, caught on the breeze
It lingers for a moment to play and to tease

Once the object of awe and fascination
A wonder to a child's mind and imagination
A simple pleasure for all to hear
Sadly not appreciated, for many a year

Now long abandoned and forgotten
Half hidden by branches in an overgrown garden
Many leaves have fallen and seasons have passed
The years have gone by some slowly, some fast

The child has long since grown and left
And tears of both sorrow and joy have been wept
The world moves faster with little time to stop and
listen
Seduced in the search for things that glitter and
glisten

But sometimes I hear it in the fluttering breeze
An echo in my mind, a memory to please
As the passing breeze just carries it along
A never-ending symphony. An ever-changing song.

The Wind of Souls

On a winter's night, dark and black as coal
The wild wind howls like a demented soul
Like a raging animal left loose from its cage
Venting it's pent-up fury and rage
Shrieking like a banshee, it screams and calls
Like a demented demon , battering against walls
Rattling the windows and knocking on doors
Ghostly footsteps on creaking floors
Not a night for humans to venture out
There are other world creatures out and about
The veil between worlds is torn and thin
God only knows what strange creatures come in
Ghostly shades and lost Spirits roam
A night to stay warm, safe and at home.
A night to snuggle up and stay in bed
And pull the blankets up to cover your head
As the storm rages against window and glass
And wait for the Wind of Souls to pass.

Cameron Morse is Senior Reviews editor at *Harbor Review* and the author of eight collections of poetry. His first collection, *Fall Risk*, won Glass Lyre Press's 2018 Best Book Award. His book of unrhymed sonnets, *Sonnetizer*, is forthcoming from Kelsay Books. He holds a Master of Fine Arts degree from the University of Kansas City-Missouri and lives in Independence, Missouri, with his wife and three children.

For more information, check him out at:

https://www.facebook.com/cameronmorsepoems
https://cameronmorsepoems.wordpress.com/

Genevieve

My unborn daughter kicks
in the window curtain. Warm air
rising from the furnace
below. A pilot light
in winter dark: a flame kept burning
continuously. Genevieve,
are you coming to continue
my story? Will I greet you only
in passing? Out here, in the living
room, I listen for the furnace.
I hold my breath, my heat trapped
under the blanket in my lap.
Behind me, down the corridor
of stars, you tread water, Mommy
waterlogged in our bed,
weighed down, and waiting. We hold
our breaths: Me with my one
lamp on, my ears perked, dialed in
to listen; she with the living word
I'm after power-kicking in her
belly before wakeup time.

Almost Dinnertime in Independence, Missouri

Meditative turn of attic turbines as winter sunset
    buries its gold
nugget in the dark bosom of the woods

minuscule white dome of half-moon waxing a silver
    tooth cap

twilight now scabs in the ambiguity of ice and old
    snow
leftover wedding cake carnage from the colossal food
    fight
of the angel roadkill of existence of the sun and dark

bald patches of earth the raw cold of unfurred fingers
numbing away with the pale light airliner cutting its
    long slow incision
across the Arctic circle of the sky C-

sectioning a second birth. Breaking the glass we
    lived under
the surface of the lake we took into our lungs.

The Ease

Ultimate autumn
turn away from the sun
into blue shadow

easier to fill up on
than stuffy heat.
There's an emptiness

to autumn, an opening
unto clear sky. There's a
kind of clarity to trees

that have given every
last leaf. The bare woods
put trains on display

in autumn. Bright
graffiti shines
in winter's glass.

Its held breath is kept
in abeyance, in
waiting
for whatever's next.

North Wind

Seethe of treetops
all of a sudden
a cauldron

a cold leviathan
surfacing long
sliver silver

fish the clouds
are floes
are fields of ice

now
there is no nuisance
no news. This dis-

quieting down-
turn is all too familiar
this question of my health

I have a reputation
for hiding under
the weather.

The North Wind
Illustration by Harrison Weir
1867

Jennifer O'Shea lives in beautiful Minnesota, a place of transforming beauty. Her writings reflect the observations and synergy between the idea of her eternal spirit and the experiences she accumulates with nature and art. She is often inspired by the Persian poet, Hafiz.

This summer she had a poem selected for inclusion in the Southern Arizona Press anthology, *The Stars and Moon in the Evening Sky*. Jennifer had three pieces chosen for a book of poems titled, Open Skies Poetry Volume 1. Most recently, one of her poems was featured in the Southern Arizona Press anthology *Ghostly Ghouls and Haunted Happenings.*

Spellbound

Enveloped in nature's wintery gift,
Feathery down floats like a dream.
A spellbinding moment I stop in awe
Maybe kindred water spirits are we.

Beguiling

A winter's walk in eve, so quiet and serene
The snowy insulation deep and white, absorbing
I feel the peace that comes as I step along the path
A moonlit moment of beguiling crystalline.

Winter Thrill

With rosy cheeks and fuzzy hats
Our joy laced echoes bounce off the hills
With sleds and skis and chasing dogs
We bound down crisscrossed paths of thrill.

Thaw

A frozen moment in wintertide
Ice coated giving nature pause
Gray clouds crawl then beams of light
Soon drips, plops, and so it thaws

D.C. Buschmann is a retired editor, teacher, and reading specialist. She has been a finalist in several poetry contests and holds a double master's degree in Education. Her poem, "Death Comes for a Friend" was the Editor's Choice in *Poetry Quarterly, Winter 2018*. Her work has been published in many journals nationally and internationally, including Kurt Vonnegut Museum and Library's *So it Goes Literary Journal*, *The Adirondack Review*, *Tipton Poetry Journal,* and *Red Coyote*. She lives in Carmel, Indiana with husband Nick and miniature schnauzers Cupcake and Coco. Her first poetry collection, *Nature: Human and Otherwise*, was published in February 2021.

Arctic Dog Walk

Arctic air
frigid like ice
bites & stings
two noses
and eight paws
surveying
the back forty
for suitable
terrain
to chow down
on nature's snow cream.

Snow—A Reminder

Snow will come and go
at its own discretion.

The wise
will surrender

to its frigid, head-strong will.

Ice Bergs

people are like ice bergs
what you see is not always
the whole picture

What Will the Birds Eat?

Wearing a foot of snow
like a high white top hat
on his naked-wood thatched roof,
the little birdhouse,
now aslant,
surrenders
to the glistering
stillness
of our backyard.
The feeder is secured,
dangling in the dip of the iron
shepherd's staff.

This is what the birds see
when they search for seed.

One ambitious cardinal, puffing
herself up into a tiny beach ball,
hunkers down on the icy
snow covered branch
beside the pole.
She catches me making out
her yellowish-tan feathers
and dazzling orange beak
through the window.
Eyes lowered,
breath held,
I about-face
with as much stealth
as I can muster.
Don't fly away. Please, please stay.
After a moment, I steal a look back.
Only her eyes move.

Honorable Mention in the 2014 Contemporary American Poetry Prizes
First published in *Journal of Modern Poetry* 17, Chicago Poetry Press
Also published in D.C. Buschmann's poetry collection:
Nature: Human and Otherwise, February 8, 2021

Mary Ellen Talley has had poems published in numerous literary journals including *Gyroscope*, *Raven Chronicles*, *Rat's Ass Review*, and *Banshee* as well as in several anthologies. A former school-based speech-language pathologist (SLP), she resides in Seattle, Washington. Her work has received three Pushcart nominations. A chapbook, *Postcards from the Lilac City* was published by Finishing Line Press in 2020.

Stay Put Under Orion's Belt

Under the circumstances, wait for rescue.
The operator reminds you not to stray
from initial GPS coordinates.
Remain warm. Walk in circles. Look at stars.
No more photos. Keep your cell line open.
Roads close yet so far. It may take two hours
for the sheriff's snowmobiles to reach you.

The new moon bright shines its blue-dark sky;
refracted constellations come into view.
Puffed-lace snowflakes fall from tall branches.
Deep warm wells of snow around trunks
of immense spruces might bury you – or
become shelter. You are the silence of quiet.
Ghosts nibble pinecones expelling Spring seeds.

Into Scottish Lakes High Camp…

We're squeezed in a Sno-Cat loaded with sleeping bags, cold weather jackets, gaiters and cross-country skis. Guest pamphlet says mice like to sneak up between floorboards to nibble on crumbs or clothing, secure food, toiletries, and luggage. Each morning we four descend a ladder to ski paths among tall evergreens that echo silence. Our son and daughter say they are touching the sky.

narrow trails meander
above tree line
sinews weave over snow

Soft fuzzy with large snowman on the front. Rusty nose, grey top hat, blue striped scarf, scattered snowflakes. I return the sweater to the backpack at night, zip it most of the way. Patch of black wool gone in the morning.

nibbled strands
warm nest
grateful mice

Seamstress in Seattle says the effort worthless
without an exact donor yarn match, unravels ribbing
along the sweater hem to gather spider threads of
matching black. One week later, hole gone, sweater
a tad shorter. Now resides in my great-great aunt's
cedar chest. My mind returns to hours gliding by as
wind gusts clouds of white across powder trails right
next to tree trunk caverns.

icicles melt
from evergreen boughs
children twist pine needle yarn into shadows

F-Stop Over Snow Angel

She may not be able to rise
gingerly to leave a snow angel intact.

What in winter's long spent vortex
is left for photographers to capture and revise?
Pink sunset over snow at Green Lake?
Baby fistfuls of white atop yellow witch hazel
    blooming early?
Yesterday's sculpted snow creature sitting on a park
    bench?
Someone's partial igloo?
Homemade moguls on an unplowed sledding street?
White-laden tree branches buried in the grass?
Icicles hanging from frozen gutters?
Hold like a popsicle. Crunch like a carrot.
Some smooth as a new leaf. Some with taste like a
    lip kiss.

She plans to capture a photo,
magic-white   cold-bite   skin-tingle!
Recipe mix glycerin plus dish soap and water,
she blows a bubble high. Lifts her camera.
Finger chill. She adjusts aperture to catch
of ice crystals dance across the floating bubble.
Freezing makes the orb opaque.
One photo will be a map of the world.
Click. Click. Quick – as her fragile planet approaches
white tufts on a leafy bush.
Not one hand will touch it to destroy wonder. Then
    poof!

Full moon swoon of the moment
into memory's vortex.

Free Skate at the Spokane Coliseum

She tucked low on the ice,
straightened right leg forward
to *shoot the duck* just inches off
and parallel to the skating surface,
    touching the ice with gloved hands,
        marring the ice with each traverse,
            chiseling air and ice with each abrupt stop,
while cold fire held her lungs tight.

When time to clean ice mid-session,
the young Zamboni driver
climbed aboard his machine to circle,
scrape each groove she had carved,
    spray new water on a smooth surface,
        climb out of his big rig,
            walk the rink's edge, checking for debris,
then beckon her back on ice through the entry gate.

Each Saturday, she stretched
to glide in backward forward figure-eights.
She played in supple spirals
until spinning twirled her vision.
    Yes, she pursued the Zamboni man.
        He might be the lasting sentry for her skating,
            fill grooves she carves – on or off the ice
   –

with a continuous film of frozen water.

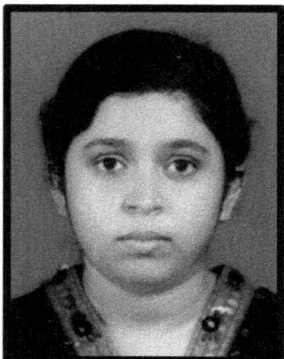

Dibyasree Nandy is a 29-year-old resident of India She began writing two years ago, after completing Master of Science and Master of Technology degrees. She has authored six books, *The Labyrinth of Silent Voices-Epistles from the Mahabharata*, *Stardust: Haiku and Other Poems*, *Studded with Rubies; A Hundred Short Stories*, *Marchen of Newer Days*, *Liebeslied*, and *Windflower*. Several of her poetry and prose pieces have appeared in literary journals and anthologies such as *The Pine Cone Review*, *Proceedings from the Pondicherry Lodge*, *Indian Periodical*, *Literary Cocktail Magazine*, *White Enso*, *Open Skies*, *Dragonflies and Fairies*, *Ghostly Ghouls and Haunted Happenings*, *Dark Reflections*, *Haus*, *Brown Sugar*, *Double Speak Magazine*, *LitGleam*, *Soul*, *Mediterranean Poetry*, *Seaglass Literary*, and *Abominable*.

Frozen in Winter's Portrait

The azure mirror pristine, unblemished;
Stream of crystal, the stillness cherished;
Pines of lapis lazuli, the turquoise woodlands dense;
Flakes of floral forms swarm as squalls commence.
On dry boughs, heaps of sprinkles;
When the icy footprints of the silver princess fall, the
    mountain wrinkles;
Not a cloud, the cerulean sky;
The mien of the heavens wry.
A rug of teal snow; the embankment;
Silent is the rill; a blue, lacquered enchantment;
The shell deflects wintry rays; diamond-like;
Inverted trees with cedar cones and many a jagged
    spike.
Pearly hillocks blinding;
Cottony, thin stems billowing;
Indigo trunks strong;
Porcelain sprays that throng.
Frosty eyelids heavy with sleep;
A dreamscape of a slate kiss on the rimy lip;
The sterling veil conjured by a pale-skinned fairy;
Inhale the serene fragrance of the unperturbed
    prairie.

Quietude of Lovely Desolation

A path to nowhere, beautifully desolate;
Silence pressing from all sides, inviting is the dark
    woody shade;
The refreshing snow choking the morning-scape;
The misty breaths of the joyous frost forming a slate-
    hued, gossamer drape.
This cheerless calm spells peace;
Yet if felled are the indigo trees;
Gloom shall disappear as light seeps in;
The onyx, murky sombreness, oh so tranquil; the
    axes, weapons of sin.
The sky not azure, but wonderfully grey;
Should pretty flakes rain down like the spear of
    Gungnir, wind swirling them away;
The harsh melody of the storm won't be rough;
The quietude of the aftermath shall be tough.
If the icy road heaped cerulean makes a crunchy
    noise;
Will you prefer that to a frozen lake meant to glide
    past, O Traveller running from your rimy soul,
    what is your choice?
Stop for a while;
You who have traipsed for many a mile.
Peer into the mirror, the body of water that has
    ceased;
Your turbulent heart, your glassy eyes… must be
    appeased;
How long have you known despair?
Enough to cross the portal to an inverted world; upon
    the tundra, your body bare?
Touch your replica;
Akin to the two stars of Spica;
Embrace your twin;

Grasp, comprehend and grin.
All shall revert, reverse;
Flipping December's white verse;
The nip in the air will always be raw;
Your desire to rush to the hearth, the comfort of the
    fiery, swallowing maw.

Wintry Dawn

A mantle of snow on firs tall;
The shy dawn peering behind the trunks as fronds
    drape themselves in a crimson shawl;
Radiance filtering through;
The frigid lake turns orange, forgetting its azure hue.
Rimy groves nigh;
Tints of peach and sweet tangerine beneath the
    mauve sky;
A veil of foggy gold;
The embankment and the glade emblazon ten-fold.
On the glistening pink ground, chalky; little birds
    perch;
Warmth they desperately search;
Bathe under the shimmering rays;
Dark plumes shall glow like the dying afternoons of
    late March days.
Vermillion sentinels, the trees stand guard;
Over the stream of crystal rainbow of many a shard;
A low tarn upon a barren range's lap;
Too tiny to register on the nation's silver map;
Yet a cross-section, a slice, a microcosm of winter's
    splendour on its own;
An alabaster zone.
A buoyant paint-brush;
The shades and tinges of the sleet-smeared months
    lush.

Winter
Von Klever
1876

Donna Nemmers is a native Iowan, who enjoys gardening, cooking, spending time with her family, and poetry. Her poem "Iris" was a winner in the 2020 International Dylan Thomas Day Poetry Competition and published by Infinity Books UK. Several of her poems on the pandemic appear in *Lockdown Literature*, published by CultureCult Magazine and Press, December 2020. Her work also appears in *Agape Review*. She has enjoyed a full career in the college textbook publishing industry, working with authors across a host of life and physical sciences disciplines.

Nature's Cloak

Crisp air foretells the long goodbye
trees shiver their vesture into north wind
earth slips on its overcoat
furred creatures scurry and burrow
a spray of gems layer into frozen shimmer
bedazzling every blade and stem and tree
until the warmth of spring
brings reawakening

Winter Vacation

Scores of winged scavengers
perhaps lost upon their route
pecking ground in dead of winter
as this pond is iced throughout

My arrival does not startle
their grazing, busily
I keep my distance to be sure
they are not pecking me

A gander puffs and spreads his wings
to warn off all the lot
to resist his horde of vagabonds
and their grassy little spot

The passing train's shrill whistle
doesn't spook away
this spacious clutch of geese
from their winter holiday

What does this tundra offer
so brown and frozen cold
for these hungry feathered wanderers
a dozen, sevenfold?

The worms have not yet wakened
into thawing springtime rain
it seems they are just nibbling
at their shadows on this plain

So maybe it's the sunshine
that provokes this ground aeration
at this little roadside stop
on this goose vacation

Window Seat

Snow-covered ridges
　　one shot from avalanche
lost in reflection
　　ten minutes of clouds pass

Slipping down below to
　　patchwork browns and reds
sewed expertly together
　　with meandering cobalt threads

Like veins in a budding leaf
　　winding streams suckle the land
puffs of smoke at first
　　clouds billow and expand

As the plane trembles above
　　snow falls inside this globe
so long, so far, so hard
　　to make the pilgrimage home

Lynn White lives in north Wales. Her work is influenced by issues of social justice and events, places, and people she has known or imagined. She is especially interested in exploring the boundaries of dream, fantasy, and reality. She was shortlisted in the Theatre Cloud 'War Poetry for Today' competition and has been nominated for a Pushcart Prize, Best of the Net, and a Rhysling Award. Her poetry has appeared in many publications including: Apogee, Firewords, Capsule Stories, Gyroscope Review and So It Goes.

Find Lynn at:

https://lynnwhitepoetry.blogspot.com
https://www.facebook.com/Lynn-White-Poetry-1603675983213077/

As Winter Falls

Willow don't weep for me.
Back in the summer
I hid in the shadows
of your leafy canopy.
Now you have left me exposed
waiting
for the winter of my content
which falls every year
as the lost leaves
turn golden
then brown
with decay
then white
with the silence
of the first snowfall.
I'm waiting for it
to blanket me with light
and make me smile.
Willow don't weep for me.

First published in Sylvia, December 2020

Winter Light

When the winter light hits the trees
the blue disappears in a spectrum
of bright white and gold
shooting out like a beaming star
from a brilliant diamond
and then fades away
fades with the sinking feeling
of an endgame approaching
as the blue disappears
swallowed by winter dark
eaten up by blackness
all too soon.

First published in Flora Fiction, Winter 2020/21

Such Fun

It was such fun to jump in autumn puddles,
that made mud spatters on my red wellies
and pale, sun starved legs,
in weather too wet to kick up the leaves
that lay swept soggily into piles.

And when winter came, such fun
to leap into snow drifts
that came over the tops of my red wellies
and my extra socks
as I tested the deepness of the snow
and the slipperiness of the ice slide.

Come the summer rain, I tried on my red wellies
but they had grown too small or me too large,
so I got my feet wet when I jumped in the stream.
Such fun, but I missed my red wellies.

First published in Midnight Circus, Fall issue 2016, EAB publishing

Elaine Reardon is a writer and herbalist. Her first chapbook, *The Heart is a Nursery For Hope*, won first honors from Flutter Press in 2016. Her second chapbook, *Look Behind You*, was published by Flutter Press in late 2019. Recently Elaine's poetry and short fiction have recently been published by Pensive Journal, Prospectus Literary, The Wild Word, and several anthologies. Elaine has had poems included in two previous Southern Arizona Press anthologies and has recently trusted Southern Arizona Press with the reprinting of her two amazing chapbooks of poetry.

Follow Elaine at:

www.elainereardon.wordpress.com.

Winter Night

I've gotten used to the sounds
deep in a winter night,
the loud crack of ice from the brook,
a sharp ping of the wood stove
reaching some new temperature,
muffled tumbles of a smoldering log,
the creak of floorboards
as if someone walked quietly.

Downstairs the refrigerator motor hums,
the water heater readjusts.
What is shifting inside this house

I wonder, content, then roll back to sleep.
The snow loosens its grip on the roof
slides with a grand whoosh,
louder than any wild animal outside.

Early Morning

From the kitchen window I watch deer
emerging from trees along the stream.
A doe wanders up the hillside, sniffing.
She digs to reveal snow-crusted juniper.

Emerging by trees along the stream
a fawn follows, soundless in the snowy field.
She digs to reveal snow-crusted juniper.
I watch from the warm side of the window.

A fawn follows, soundless in the snowy field
The deer startles at the sound of my mug set down
I watch from the warm side of the window.
My guests eat dry grass and juniper; I have coffee.

They look up at the sound of my mug on the table.
The doe wanders up the hillside, sniffing.
My guests eat dry grass and juniper; I have coffee.
From the kitchen window I watch deer.

Previously published in *Look Behind You* (Flutter Press, 2016)

Winter Storm

Branches crack under the weight of snow
cold wind pushes hard against bowing trunks
pine forest sways and moans
diamonds fall as limbs shiver

wind pushes against bowing trunks
a groan sounds deep in heartwood
diamonds fall as limbs shiver
heaped snow rests discarded
like nightclothes in early morning light

a groan sounds deep in heartwood
Winds shift snow weighing branches down
heaped snow rests discarded
like nightclothes in early morning light
silence   aside from a tomcat's howl

winds shift snow weighing branches down
abiding until light.
silence   aside from a tomcat's howl
in the stillness a moon sliver appears

fox curls hidden   waits for dawn
pine forest sways and moans
in the stillness a moon sliver appears
branches crack under the weight of snow

Previously published in *Look Behind You* (Flutter Press, 2016)

Alice Pero is the tenth Poet Laureate of Sunland Tujunga. Her first published book, *Thawed Stars* was praised by Kenneth Koch as having "clarity and surprises." Her second book, *Sunland Park Poems* was a collaboration with Elsa Frausto. *Beyond Birds and Answers* is an ekphrastic work with New York City artist, Vera Campion. Pero's poems have been published in many magazines and anthologies including *Wide Awake, Coiled Serpent, San Diego Poetry Annual, Pratik, Nimrod, National Poetry Review Spillway, and G.W. Review*. She is the Monthly Contest Chair of the California State Poetry Society. Having taught poetry to children since 1991, she considers it her mission to keep poetry and creativity alive in the generations and many of her students' poems have been published in California Poets in the Schools anthologies. An accomplished flutist and former dancer, Pero is also the founder of Moonday, a reading series which has been on-going in the Los Angeles area since 2002 and Windsong Players Chamber Ensemble, which performs regularly around Los Angeles. A passionate dialoguer, she has created poetry dialogues with over 25 poets. She lives in Sunland with her husband, Dennis, on the edge of the desert wash.

Follow her at: www.alicepero.com

Snow I

Under the expanse of snow
the field lies brown and hard
Virgin beauty in reluctant
dormancy
It lies and waits

Under the shallow mantle
of complacency
I yield
wanting to be heard
The surging of my blood stopped
in stasis
I lie and ache

And who will push the bound up
earth apart
and break the clods
the winter froze
And who will urge
the pounding of my heart?

Previously published in *Thawed Stars* (Sunlink Publications)

Snow II

The snow makes the earth mumble
No more sharp, well enunciated creaks
The birds' shrieks are muffled
into soft crinkles of sound
The blanket wraps bundles
of houses cars
Huddles them into quiet
A million particles of white
insulate the thunder
cushion the sharp edges of night

The snow makes silence right
A soundless expanse of serenity
covering every corroded part
in mute purity you can't see
but feel
Snow makes the earth fumble to move
suspends all thoughts of weeping
leaves us dumb and voiceless
in momentary innocence

Previously published in *Thawed Stars* (SunInk Publications)

Wanting Winter

When leaves fall, trip over one another,
like old ladies scrambling for corned beef hash
at the cafeteria

When leaves crumble underfoot,
a brown dessert,
children rake piles, scuffling and yelling

When they run indoors for hot chocolate,
press faces against cool autumn windows

When dying leaves lie low,
mumble to bare tree trunks,
the cold coming

You hope for hills of snow
silence to put poems in
the long stretch of winter
breathing with you

Joan McNerney is originally from New York City and now resides in the dank woodlands of upstate New York. She has been the recipient of three scholarships. She has recited her work at the National Arts Club, New York City, State University of New York, Oneonta, McNay Art Institute, San Antonio and the University of Houston, Texas as well as other distinguished venues. A reading in Treadwell, New York was sponsored by the American Academy of Poetry. She was recently named the second place winner in Wilda Morris Challenge.

Published worldwide in over 35 countries. Her work has appeared in literary publications too numerous to mention. She has been awarded four Best of the Net nominations.

The Muse in Miniature and *Love Poems for Michael* are both available on Amazon.com and Cyberwit.net. Just released is a new title *At Work*. This collection shows colorful but realistic snapshots of working women and men in their daily lives.

Blizzard

O wonderful emergency!

Silver needles spin for hours
weaving tapestries to drape
rooftops sidewalks streets.
Millions of icicles delicately
arranged on lamp posts
along metal railings
around cornices.

White magic prayed for by children.
A spell shutting down school
making way for snow fights.

A perfect opportunity to burrow
longer in bed. Be late for work
appearing unprofessional in
rough clothes.

Snow crystals cover all
stains and blemishes.
Each windowpane
becomes a
miniature museum
of fine line etchings.

We are snapped awake by frost.
Our woolen gloves full of lace.

Winter Time

Ice blue mountains
Wind swept skies.
There are always these...

And you standing
silent as the sun
burning through
this day.
You are my sun
my heaven on earth.

You bring bright ribbons
handfuls of crystal
to fasten my hair.

Stay with me this
long evening. I will
hide in your arms away
from ice blue winds.
We will be warm together.

Winter Solstice

Hurry, short days are here,
too much to do.
Get ready, find gloves,
hats, scarves, sweaters.

Stopping to see the
shape of a snowflake.

Hurry home to luxuriate
in dim light listening
to heat hissing finding
warmth from hot teas.

Bundled in bed comforted by
mounds of blankets, books.

Finally succumbing to
our northern goddess,
whose black nights are long
and silent as evergreens.

Thomas Zampino has been a Manhattan attorney for over 35 years and started writing poetry only recently. Some of his works have appeared in The University of Chicago's *Memoryhouse Magazine*, *Silver Birch Press*, *Bard's Annual 2019, 2020, 2021, and 2022, Trees in a Garden of Ashes*, *Otherwise Engaged*, *Chaos, A Poetry Vortex*, *Nassau County Voices in Verse*, and *No Distance Between Us*. Brazilian director and actor Gui Agustini produced a video enactment of his poem *Precise Moment*. His first book of poetry, *Precise Moment*, was published in 2021. He lives in New York.

He can be followed at:

https://thomaszampino.wordpress.com/

Snow Angels

Spring rains will soon clear away the last of the snow
    angels
Not that there was anything left of them but the
    memories
The five year old and the two year old bundled up
    under
Mom's orders: hats, mittens, snow pants, six layers
    thick
Carefree days that were really so only in crazy
    hindsight
Worries loomed just as large back then as they do
    today
Winter clothes long ago outgrown, but not the fears
    over
Wounds and hurts and broken hearts that can't be
    fixed
Still, I wouldn't exchange these days with anyone
    else
They remind me of carefree times that were never so
Spring rains will soon clear away the last of the snow
    angels
Not that there was anything left of them but the
    memories

Two Paths

I cleared a path to the pond this morning, the one in my backyard.

The top layer of snow had mostly melted by the time I reached the edge of the just barely frozen water. But the exercise had done me some good, reminding me, as it did, of younger days when I was eager to earn a dollar or two from the neighbors. Sometimes scoring a cup of hot chocolate in the process.

It feels as if this will be the last storm of the season. Spring is just weeks away and the weather forecast is already forging its own path towards warmer days ahead. But mostly, it's been an unusually mild winter here in the northeast. Hardly any time at all given over to thoughts of hibernation, death, resurrection, or renewal.

I can't say that I'll much miss the cold. But a part of me still wants to mourn it like I would the passing of an old acquaintance. All the better to welcome spring with its yet unsullied promises, I suppose.

But for now, I'll stand here just long enough to enjoy my own path-clearing artistry.

And think back on some days long since gone.

The Winter Sun

Who can know the sound of frost melting in the
     winter sun?
Or the scent of buried seeds waiting for the spring?
I sometimes think of love that way.
Imperceptible, yet palpable.
Innocent, yet profane.

Mark Andrew Heathcote is adult learning difficulties support worker. He has poems published in journals, magazines, and anthologies both online and in print. He resides in the United Kingdom and is from Manchester. Mark is the author of *In Perpetuity* and *Back on Earth*, two books of poems published by Creative Talents Unleashed.

It's so bewildering

Dawn in the wintertime is like a coffin-lid
lifted and, a feldspar of bones shimmering
ice-covered reaches out to touch your hands.
Ice crystals bear their impressive teeth, mouth-
crammed
it's so bewildering and embittering
-yet enriching, splashing about snow like a squid.

The world flickers into life; turned ghostly white
shrubs are buckling with weight, not of their own.
trees, like the horses of the apocalypse
-stand frozen, mid-gallop, and stars like steamships?
Glisten orange like a flower overblown,
petals near spilling like a meteorite.

I'd pluck the stars for flowers

If I could bathe in dew with you
capture a snowdrop longingly
descending on or amid our two
pursed pressed lips, turning blue.

If I could, I'd freeze this time
for all our immortality,
and I'd love you only
I'd adore the wintertime.

Those bewitching shivers on your breath
I'd pluck the stars for flowers
I'd weave them like a moonbeams thread
in silken ribbons silver for you.

I'd keep these memories
till the world and all its miseries,
were once and finally all dead
if I could, only love you.

Winter Séances

Life's forgotten how to smile.
Its little winter séances—
set a scene of bewilderment
like mistletoes bedraggled penance.

The dramatization waits.
Kneeling behind every tuft
awakening behind every hedgerow.
'Hibernation is slowly rebuffed.'

Life again begins to smile.
And birds sing in the valley
and spread mistletoe,
by their scraggy toes so happily.

Death, on the contrary, frowns
where the thistle downs
rise and fall jauntily.
Here a rainbow alights atop the clouds.

And entire fields of flower
ringing in their golden heads
turn to see us in our trampling steps
that has thrown aback their winding bedspreads.

Jerri Hardesty lives in the woods of Alabama with husband, Kirk, who is also a poet. They run the nonprofit poetry organization, New Dawn Unlimited, Inc. (NewDawnUnlimited.com). Jerri has had over 500 poems published and has won more than 1600 awards and titles in both written and spoken word poetry.

Cryogenics

Icy breath
Of frozen night sighs,
Exhales slow-falling snow,
Frosts the windows
Like cataract eyes,
Tucks in the city
Under blanket of white.

Aerodynamics

Clasping his mother's hand, the child
Bravely stepped out onto the ice.
The thin blades of the skates
Slipped away,
Threatened to slide out
From under him completely,
But her strong grip
Lifted him up,
Kept him on his feet
Until he regained his balance.
They circled the rink,
Hand in hand,
Until his skills improved,
His ankles learning
The tipping point between
The flex and the rigidity
That kept him gliding
Round and round.
And then, she let go,
Releasing this fledgling
To soar on his own,
Arms stretched out like wings
Capturing the winds
Of his first flight.

Previously published in Peninsula Poets, 2012

Treats

Winter's icy breath
Sugar coats fluffy pine trees,
Making eye candy,
Icicles are popsicles,
Bushes are powdered donuts.

LaVern Spencer McCarthy has written and published nine books, five of poetry and four of fiction.

Her work has appeared in *Writers and Readers Magazine*, *Meadowlark Reader*, Agape Review, *Fenechty Publications Anthologies Of Short Stories*, *From The Shadows*, *An Anthology Of Short Stories*, *Visions International*, and others. She is a life member of The Poetry Society Of Texas and National Federation of State Poetry Societies, Inc.

She resides in Blair, Oklahoma where she is currently writing her fifth book of short stories.

LaVern had poems featured in two previous Southern Arizona Press anthologies and we are delighted to have two of her works included in this anthology.

Sounds Of Winter

I love the sounds of snowy days--
the crackle in the atmosphere--
the footsteps squeaking on the glaze.
I love the sounds of snowy days,
the cardinal in cheerful praise--
his melody so sweet and clear.
I love the sounds of snowy days,
the crackle in the atmosphere.

Down Winter's Way

Come walk down winter's way with me.
when leaves have fallen, one by one.
Pretend that April cannot be.
How beautiful, the waning sun!

When leaves have fallen, one by one one,
we'll cheer that summer said goodbye.
How beautiful, the waning sun!
Too soon the light will fade and die.

We'll cheer that summer said goodbye
when all things wild have swiftly flown.
Too soon the light will fade and die,
the earth will sleep through days unknown.

When all things wild have swiftly flown,
we shall be happy till the spring.
the earth, will sleep through days unknown
in sleet and snow the moments bring.

We shall endure until the spring.
Pretend that April cannot be
In sleet and snow the moments bring,
come walk down winter's way with me.

Lennart Lundh is a poet, photographer, short-fictionist, and historian living in Orland Hills, Illinois. His work has appeared internationally since 1965.

.

The lady who lives in the woods

is getting along in age, though not as much as if
she'd lived these years in the city, where life would
have been softer and her body long on aches
squatting on the unused landscape. She dresses
warmer now for the months of chill and damp, favors
shade when the heat is full, sleeps well but rises
early to make the most of Time's more reckless
speed. The years for raising foals are long behind,
the needs and memories of mares and stallions
settled if not yet dusty, and so she takes an old
gelding to shape, to work with, training it to her ways.
There's white snow on the ground today, gray mist in
the air beneath the hidden sun. Her companion's
coat shines as bright and neat as hers is dark and
right, as both their breaths are clear and clean with
the effort made to be together.

Inspired by the 1899 photograph *The Horse Trainer*, by Félix
Thiollier.

Previously published in *Poems Against Cancer 2021* (self-
published chapbook to raise funds for the St. Baldrick's
Foundation)

The Horse Trainer
Félix Thiollier, 1899

Rp Verlaine lives in New York City. He has a Master of Fine Arts in creative writing from City College. He taught in New York Public schools for many years. His first volume of poetry, Damaged by Dames & Drinking, was published in 2017 and another, Femme Fatales Movie Starlets & Rockers, in 2018. A set of three e-books titled Lies From The Autobiography vol 1-3 were published from 2018 to 2020. His newest book, Imagined Indecencies, was published in February of 2022.

Flight Of Birds

Summer long gone,
we walk the thin ice
till she needs more space.

She, who dared me
to enter her thoughts,
leaves nothing unturned

The freezing chill
we can traipse past,
not the chasm between us.

All through the fall
she spoke of the birds
leaving her behind

Now it's my turn,
watching the snow melt,
her leave with suitcase.

Joseph A. Farina is a retired lawyer in Sarnia, Ontario, Canada. An internationally award-winning poet. Several of his poems have been published in Quills Canadian Poetry Magazine, The Wild Word, The Chamber Magazine, Lothlorian Poetry Journal, Ascent, Subterranean Blue, The Tower Poetry Magazine, Inscribed, The Windsor Review, Boxcar Poetry Revue, and appear in many anthologies including: Sweet Lemons: Writings with a Sicilian Accent, Canadian Italians at Table, Witness from Serengeti Press, and Tamaracks: Canadian Poetry for the 21st Century. He has had poems published in the U.S. magazines Mobius, Pyramid Arts, Arabesques, Fiele-Festa, Philedelphia Poets and Memoir (and). He has had two books of poetry published, The Cancer Chronicles and The Ghosts of Water Street.

He has had poetry published in three Southern Arizona Press anthologies.

aspects of a winter's day

i
on a cold winter morning
in the blue light
frost-tinged trees shine

ii
faded evergreens
greying in artic winds
shedding

iii
the strangling frigid hands of ice
claw at windows
in fillagree fingers

iv
the scene is one of pantomime
ice snow winter wind
lifeless white shadows

v
the only movement
ice flows and circles
on gelating river currents

long winter

this winter's lasting too long
and I miss that you're not here
the fireplace is crackling
it's a warm and sleepy atmosphere
reminding me of Sunday mornings
waking to freshly fallen snow
and the sparkling of the sunlight
off its crystalline sheeting
I've got new poetry to read you
by the fire with soft music
and I miss that you're not here

Jo Barbara Taylor lives in Raleigh, North Carolina, where she writes poetry and fiction, and leads writing workshops. Her wring has appeared in journals, magazines, anthologies, and online. She has published four poetry books with small presses.

Winterscape

Frost calls forth small complaints—
　　Aunty Scrap's stiff joints, cold feet—
　　our secret regrets.

A freeze uncovers Martha's skates.
　　She bends and leaps on the stainless pond,
　　lands, then skates backward
　　in the flawless flow of arms and legs.

The first snow prompts the usual platitude:
　　every snowflake a unique design. We watch
　　flakes
　　drift across the road, worry about losing power.
　　Each of us remembers a snowier time,
　　and the house grows cozy with stories.

　　　　Mama tells how Grandma got lost in a
　　　　　　blizzard.
　　　　Grandpa came across her, frostbitten and
　　　　blinded by the snow. He carried her to a
　　　　barn, laid her next to a cow. Grandma
　　　　always said she married him because he
　　　　knew a prize heifer when he saw one.

　　　　Aunty Scrap says she fell in a snowdrift one
　　　　dark night, flat on her back. She waggled a
　　　　snow angel, and clouds parted like the Red
　　　　Sea. Then a winter moon lit the sky, and
　　　　she posed angelic in the light, a field of
　　　　diamonds all around her.

Grandpa recites a ghost tale: a crooked man
    toted a leather poke through a snowstorm,
    heavy with things of this world. The
    stranger limped, bent forward at the waist;
    left hand withered, eyepatch over one eye.
    After the storm in melted snow, a humble
    crone found the poke with lilies and lotus
    blossoms spilling out. The eyepatch lay on
    the ground; no other sign of the man until
    the following winter when a robust fellow
    strode the highway waving, waving to
    folks. As he came close, they could see
    the hollow eye socket staring through
    purple scurf and pus. Everyone hid except
    the old woman. She laid the snow lily
    against his temple. A tear fell on her hand.
    His blue eye looked upon her, young and
    comely, and they danced across snow
    stars to the moon.

When frost forecasts winter,
    Aunty Scrap says *I never see a white lily that I*
    don't thank my lucky stars for diamond-strewn
    snow. Oh, I wish I'd snow-angeled all the way
    home that night.

Ken Allan Dronsfield is a disabled veteran and prize-winning poet from New Hampshire, now residing in Oklahoma. He has six poetry collections to date. Ken's been nominated four times for the Pushcart Prize and seven times for Best of the Net. He worked with friend Michael Lee Johnson as Co Editor for three print anthologies, *Moonlight Dreamers in Yellow Haze*, *Dandelion in a Vase of Roses* and *Warriors With Wings*. He was First Prize Winner for the 2018 *and* 2019, Realistic Poetry International Nature Poetry Contests. Ken loves writing, thunderstorms, coin collecting, and spending time with his rescue cats Willa and Yumpy.

That Tinge of Winter

The old barn moans and groans as
my bones creak on this frosty day.
Roaming into now harvested fields
the maze now but stubble and husk
I watch as the winds conspire with
bare branches to tickle a setting sun.
From darkening clouds floating above,
a lone snowflake drifts slowly down
stinging the tip of my cold red nose.
Twilight time chases the day away
here, by the now bare apple trees
near a haunted wood, winter smiles.

John Anthony Fingleton was born in Cork City, in the Republic of Ireland. He has lived in many countries including the UK, France, Mexico as well as six tours to different states in Africa, during service with the French Armed Forces and is now living in Paraguay, South America. His poems have been published in journals and anthologies in Ireland, UK, USA, India, and France as well as three produced plays. Poems read on Irish and American radio as well in Spanish on South American broadcasts. He has contributed to four books of poetry for children. He has poems published in *Spillwords, Alien Bhudda, The Red Door, Piker Press, Super Poetry Highway, The Writers Magazine, Ariel Chart,* and numerous national and international journals, blogs, reviews, and anthologies. He was named Poet of the Year (2016) for the Destiny Poets International Community, Poet of the Month (March 2019) Our Poetry Archive, Poet of the Month (April 2019) The League of Poets, Author of the Month (December 2020) *Spillwords,* and nominated for Author of the Year *Spillwords* 2020. His published collections include: *Poems from the Shadowlands* (November 2017), *Words That Found Me* (December 2019), *Poems From The Banks* (January 2020), *Poems from a Restricted Place (*April 2020), *Secret Fjords (*May 2020), *A Gathering Of Words* (June 2020), and *Lost Places and Other Poems* (January 2021). All which are available on Amazon.

Late Snows

Sometimes I fail to see the flowers,
Or the blossoms on the trees;
Sometimes I do not hear the songbirds
Or the breeze rustling through the leaves.
My mind takes in artificial things,
That always disappears,
But every time that happens,
The snows are late that year.

Sometimes I do not see the beauty
Of a raging savage sea,
Sometimes I do not listen
To the words that a love one says to me.
My mind becomes a captive,
Of things I do not wish to hear,
But every time that happens,
The snows are late that year.

Wintering Out

What will you do now, my friend?
That the winter storms have come;
And the mountain pass is blocked by heavy snow.
Will you ride down to the lower plains?
And camp there for a while,
Waiting for the coming of the thaw.

If you wish, you can stay with me,
In my cabin by the lake;
It's the first year I'll be wintering out alone,
There's food and drink for more than one, and I like
    your company,
I have sacks of oats and plenty straw
For your horse, out in the barn.

I know you like the open road,
With freedom in your face;
And your nomads blood, does not like to rest too
    long,
But we can make the best of things,
While remembering old times,
Share some jokes, and sing a few sad songs.

We will not be disturbed there,
When the North road comes under snow,
Except for two wild swans nesting in the reeds,
I fear that one has died this year,
I have only seen the cob,
In many ways he's a little just like me.

You say that you must carry on?
Ok my friend, I understand,
May the road rise and the wind be to your back;
I wish I could accompany you,
But I've lost the will to go-
From now on, memories, are the only roads I'll track.

Binod Dawadi is from Purano Naikap 13, Kathmandu, Nepal. He has completed his master's degree from Tribhuvan University in English and enjoys reading and writing in literary forms, creating many poems and stories. His hobbies include reading, writing, singing, watching movies, traveling, and gardening as well as spending time with his pets. He is a creative person who does not spend his time by doing nothing; always helping those less fortunate. He believes that through writing and art it is possible to change the knowledge and perspectives of the people towards anything. He loves his country Nepal and has experienced the many cultures of his country as well as those of foreign countries.

His stories and poems have appeared in many anthologies and he has published his own poetry books: *The Power Of Words, Love and Life's Difficulties,* and *Nature, Animals and Human Beings* in Prodigy Published.

Holidays Of Winter

We have got a long holiday,
We will visit to the different,
Parts of the world,
We will play in the snows,
We will play boating,
We will go in the peaceful nature,
We two lovers will be only there,
We will kiss each other in our lips,
We will hold each other so much tightly,
We will give a charming smile,

We will look into,
Each other eyes,
We will forget about the time,
When day and night finishes,
We will make tea and coffee,
We will drink them,
By looking at the animals of snow,
We will look the white mountains,
We will be so much happier,
Then we had in our life in our past,

We will forget cold and winter,
From our true and spiritual love,
You don't worry if I hadn't any wealth also,
My wealth is this nature my greatest wealth,
Is this I can give for you,
Why will you worry?
My lover it will give you,
More happiness then other wealth,
So, my lover spent your time with me,
In holidays of winter.

Mark Fleisher recently published his fourth book of poetry – *Incidental Moments: New and Selected Poems*. His poetry and prose have been published in online and print anthologies in the United States, Canada, United Kingdom, Nigeria, Kenya, and India. He received a journalism degree from Ohio University and worked as a reporter and editor at newspapers in upstate New York and Washington, D.C. His time in the United States Air Force included a year in Vietnam as a combat news reporter. He was awarded a Bronze Star for meritorious service. The native of Brooklyn, New York is based in Albuquerque, New Mexico.

A Silent Night

Winter night
stars still
moon silent
wind hushed
hear snowflakes
fall on frozen ground
almost

Tracks of rabbits,
deer, maybe coyote,
embedded without
a whisper on
white blankets
window panes opaque
with coats of stealthy frost
all sounds suspended
in midnight chill

Winter Words, Winter Gifts

Stretches of brutal cold
should not shock us;
below zero, wind chill,
single digits unspoken
during other seasons
spill from our mouths,
words seemingly
suspended in morning's rime

Visitors descend
from nearby hills,
foraging for food
now scarce in the
clutches of winter
A quartet of cackling crows
takes up residence
atop a maple tree,
its branches laid bare
by swirling winds

She warns me
of cabin fever,
do not hibernate
in your cozy lair,
get out, see people,
her admonishments
arriving from
snugness and smugness
basking in the warmth
of the Southwest desert
while I shiver at
a three-figure heating bill

Feeling her love,
hearing her laughter
gladdens my heart,
warms my soul
as I endure winter's siege

Ross Leishman lives in Dunedin, at the bottom of the South Island of New Zealand, with his wife Shelley, their three children, Darceah, Bryn, and Bonnie, and their two dogs, cat, and turtle. He is the Head Chef and Food Service Manager at Tolcarne Boarding where they cater for and look after 155 Boarding school girls. He has a liking for Italian scooters and motorcycling and loves music. His influencers would be Jeff Buckley, Rodney Crowell, John Hiatt, Lana Del Rey, and Tom Petty.

He actually wrote his first poem for an English project at high school when he was 16. It was called "Sitting on a Beach" and he still remembers it word for word. Sadly, that's where his writing creativity stopped or ... paused. Fast forward to 2009. He had recently separated from his wife and children and was living alone. Misery loves company and so he started writing again, it was a great way of getting those pesky dark demons out of his head and onto paper where they belong.

Now at 52, he has gotten older and greyer and has become more comfortable and confident sharing his soul with whoever wants to see it. His life has been full of ups and downs, but he finds the most inspiration in the darker, tragic things, events in life, those dark melancholy thoughts. He writes about what he sees, what he feels, and what he hears. A couple of years ago he started doing this little introduction before each poem; "freshly deposited into tins and baked at 180 degrees in the bread bakers' oven of his mind", for example, and its sort of become his trademark.

Recently he has been privileged to be included in the *Open Skies Poetry Anthology Volume 1* and hopes to someday soon have his own collection published, watch out for *Lost Thinker - Word Alchemy*.

Winters Call

Lost in its early darkness,
mesmerized by the fires rhythmic rendition of flames of our
lives.
The weekend is welcomed by a gentle pattering of the rain
on the old tin roof, relaxing, thought provoking,
the promise of a warm, toasty all enveloping comfy bed
is too much to ignore....
as I slowly nod off to the dulcet tones of Allan Titchmarsh's
love your garden, winter is here, don't fear it, embrace it.

Winter on Fifth Avenue
Alfred Stieglitz
1892

Sandeep Kumar Mishra is the poetry editor at *Indian Poetry Review*. He has received Readers Favorite Award - 21, Indian Achievers Award - 21, IPR Poetry Award - 2020 and Literary Titan Book Award -2020. He was shortlisted for 2021 International Book Awards, 52nd New Millennium Award-2021, Asian Anthology-2021, Joy B Poetry Prize 2021, Oprelle Poetry Prize 2021, MPT Story Award-2022, Newcastle Story Award-2022, and Anasi Story Award-2022.

Winter

In snowy unpigmented drape wintry withdrawn
world waits for the warm kiss of the day,
Through the long lonely valley
the elevation blows the glacial gale
to cheer the deep and solemn solitude

Over the bare upland, a pious sunbeam
plays when the heartless west extends its blast
but the stormy north sings sleet,
All the field lay bound beneath
a crispy integument of snow,
It withers all in silence to expose the earth
and show its susceptible skeleton life

I walk to crash crunch beneath my feet
to see a dancing darkness in vivid blue,
In an ecstasy the earth drinks
the lukewarm silver sunlight,
The beast or bird in their covert rest,
These leafless trees resemble my fate,
as a lonely robin with its burning breast
sits in subtle sweetness of the sun

How ruby banner of poppies spread
where the lilies fell asleep but
the rose's hearts are beating still,
When the fresh sap of earth
finesse the flaxen flowers,
The snowflakes swarmed in the yard
to beat the feeble window panel

When, I step in warm chamber,
I wonder how like me
the grief worn threshold stone was?
Distorted and shivering shadows upon
the dim lighted ceiling,
The colourless clusters of lacklustre stars
ornaments the night bride,
The lenient liquid moon slides
through bare black branch

A chamber corner draft swept the night stand
The cruciform contour of winged craving
took a fleety flash flight,
I swear to keep every sweet promise
under a warm furry blanket of seed prospect,
God pity all those homeless souls

Gregg Shapiro is the author of eight books including the poetry chapbook *Fear of Muses* (Souvenir Spoon Books, 2022). Recent/forthcoming lit-mag publications include *The Penn Review*, *Book of Matches*, *Exquisite Pandemic*, *RFD*, *Gargoyle*, *Limp Wrist*, *Mollyhouse*, *Jasper's Folly*, *Poetic Medicine*, *Impossible Archetype*, *Red Fern Review*, *The Pine Cone Review*, and *South Florida Poetry Journal*, as well as the anthologies *Let Me Say This: A Dolly Parton Poetry Anthology* (Madville Publishing, 2023), *Proud to Be: A Pride Poetry Collection* (Red Penguin, 2022), *Moving Images: Poems Inspired by Film* (Before Your Quiet Eyes Publishing, 2021), *This Is What America Looks Like* (Washington Writers' Publishing House, 2021) and *Sweeter Voices Still: An LGBTQ Anthology From Middle America* (Belt Publishing, 2021). An entertainment journalist, whose interviews and reviews run in a variety of regional LGBTQ+ and mainstream publications and websites, Shapiro lives in South Florida with his husband Rick and their dog Coco.

Lake-Effect

Half a block in from the lake, it snows here before
    anywhere
else. The dog whimpers, licks her leash, gives me a
    sideways

glance. She looks out the sunporch window, chin
    resting on
the sill. Wet, black nose pressed to the cold,
    smudged glass,
watching snow cover branches, cars and window
    ledges.

Now she wants to mess it up; leave her pawprints on
    the front
steps, the sidewalk, the palette of undisturbed
    parkway.

Previously published in *Impossible Archetype*

`79

At the end of the fourth month of winter, a season
that flexed and stretched unnecessarily from early
November through the last day of March, snowflakes
fat as frosting slapped the ground like an insult.
You feel like a figurine trapped inside of a shaken

snow-globe, unsteady and voiceless, peppered
in precipitation. You imagine shovels and bags
of salt, hastily packed away too soon by those
annoyed, desperate for a sign of change, dancing
together animatedly like characters in a vintage

Disney cartoon. Boots in closets do the same.
Thirty years earlier, by the end of that cruelest
of winters, people proudly wore buttons emblazoned
with "Snow Survivor: Chicago 1979." It provided
another legendary snowfall story to bore themselves

and future generations. Ruthless and toxic, record
levels of snow, sleet and ice crippled the city and
outlying areas, bent the communal spirit of citizens
known for their hearty Midwestern stock. Shorter
memories don't dwell on the damage, the cost

and the caustic potholes that threaten to swallow
trucks, whole city blocks. Summer's ability
to erase the pain hangs in the balance. Secretly,
summer covets winter's bad boy reputation,
the hurt that it inflicts, the scars seen and unseen.

Previously published in the chapbook *GREGG SHAPIRO: 77*
(Souvenir Spoon Books)

Marianne Tefft is a poet, lyricist, and voiceover artist who daylights as a Montessori teacher on the Dutch Caribbean island of Sint Maarten. Her poems appear in print and online journals and anthologies in the U.S., Canada, India, Serbia, and Sint Maarten. She is the author of the poetry collections *Full Moon Fire: Spoken Songs of Love* (Tellwell Talent, June 2022) and *Moonchild: Poems for Moon Lovers* (coming in December 2022).

Her work is available on Facebook (Marianne Tefft - Poet & Wordsmith)
https://www.facebook.com/MarianneTefftPoetWordsmith
and YouTube (Marianne Tefft)
https://www.youtube.com/channel/UCALiRAX7idctDYEZOUhy-eQ

Tropical Winter

At last the stagnant heat has broken
After a season of fractured dreams
Fresh breeze ruffles the lagoon
And we doze through the night
No longer rising to bathe at midnight
In the cool moonset
We reclaim the simple pleasures
That the solstice brings
As we draw a sheet to our hips
Or lift a pareo from the foot of the bed
To wrap bare shoulders
Against the Christmas winds

Carl "Papa" Palmer of Old Mill Road in Ridgeway, Virginia, lives in University Place, Washington. He is retired from the military and Federal Aviation Administration enjoying life as "Papa" to his grand descendants and being a Franciscan Hospice volunteer. Carl is president of the Puget Sound Poetry Connection in Tacoma.

PAPA's MOTTO: Long Weekends Forever!

Snow Snakes of Pina County

Not the inviting cotton candy snow
scene on a holiday greeting card
or sparkling fluffy flakes floating
softly in the shaken crystal globe,

These wind whipped ice shards blown,
thrown, stinging, not sticking, hurled,
swirled across bare brown ground like
long white snakes slithering in the sand.

Bruce E. Whitacre's debut poetry collection, *The Elk in the Glade: The World of Pioneer and Painter Jennie Hicks*, is forthcoming from Crown Rock Media. His chapbook, *Good Housekeeping*, will be out in 2023 from Poets Wear Prada. His poems have appeared in *Big City Lit, RFD, Impossible Archive, North of Oxford, Pensive Journal*, Poets Wear Prada's The Rainbow Project (nominated for Best of the Net), and *World Literature Today*. His work is included in the anthologies *American Graveyard, Brownstone Poets 2021*, and *I Wanna be Loved by You: Poems on Marilyn Monroe,* as well as the craft book, *The Strategic Poet*.

Follow him at www.brucewhitacre.com.

Winter Sky Master

Blades scour and clatter on rippled ice.
Ashore, fires blaze and puff their signal smoke.
Beneath a cloud-streaked sky,
black trees, white hills skim parti-coated people.

A hockey puck skitters between skates.
Older boys shunt and riot past.
A jagged crack catches his pointed blades
but he twirls through easily.

Balance, smarts, and strength
make skating a complex art
Yet if a kid can master this,
can't he also, calculus, or Beowulf?

Back at night under a frosty moon
ice booms in the purple air.
Perfection traces every swoosh as
skates draw the world he wills.

City lights from the valley below
cast upon the clouds a pinkish radiance.
Between their bellies twinkle stars,
Mars, Venus, and that chip of moon.

He stops short, breathless in a crystal vortex.
the sheer ice reflects the pink clouds, the stars.
Heaven and lake compress into a kiss
cold breath, hot blood, still mind,

All.

Previously included in *Seasons at the Lake* by Bruce E.
Whitacre

The View

Bonsai framed in window. Falling
snow dapples courtyard,
balletic. Chernobyl winter brims ledges,
blunts prospects from anywhere.
Kitchen clock tick tock—Covid, day 1000.

Kerri Merriam-Buckton is a Canadian author of several genres. She has had short stories and poems published in anthologies by Dark Rose Press, Ravens Quoth Press, and Sweety Cat Press. She has also self-published two books, her first novel, *Where the Trees Know You*, and a collection of her poems and photography, *The Inner Voice: A Collection of Poetry and Photography*. When she's not writing she devotes her time to her husband and three children, loves taking photos of anything that catches her eye, and dreams of travelling the world to discover new stories and inspirations.

She can be followed on:
Website: kerrimbuckton.com
Instagram: @kerrimbuckton.author

Winter Musings

The first sting of winter is in the air.
Dark, full clouds hang waiting there.
The icy chill makes me shiver,
Around me, nature starts to wither.
Leaves underfoot once high and proud,
Are slowly covered by their white shroud.
A cover while they return to earth,
And spring comes forth with their rebirth.
Now a world both grey and light,
Comes to shorten day and lengthen night.
We may be plagued with a sense of woe,
And hate the coming return of snow,
But just think of the beautiful sight,
Of snow sparkling in the light.
Like tiny diamonds on the ground,
And nights with still quiet the only sound.
There is beauty in that silence,
Or in evergreens flourishing in defiance.
Even as we dread howling nights,
And pull our coats around us, tight.
So, I hope you're able to find a reason,
To enjoy this next upcoming season.
Or at least grin, bear, and get through,
Until the warmth returns to you.

Winter's Forgiveness

The snow is rising more and more,
Erasing footprints from before.
Gently it floats, lightly touches the ground,
Softly landing without a sound.
Barely touching the flakes below,
We hardly notice it start to grow.
Ice encrusts things in its pockets,
Like photos inside lover's lockets.
Encased inside until ready to be seen,
And it is time that they are freed.
Yet it has our forgiveness on days like these,
When its beauty is all that we can see.
We still look forward to the spring ahead,
But right now, we enjoy the moment instead.
For now, the wind has lessened, is still,
And winter now seems only downhill.
The birds have again begun their song,
And it no longer seems so long.

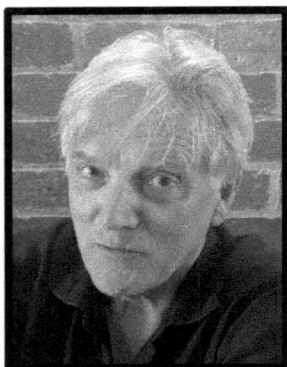

Allan Lake is a poet, originally from Allover, Canada, who now writes in Allover, Australia.

His latest collection, *My Photos of Sicily*, was published by Ginninderra Press contains no photos, only poems.

ic
ic
l
e

clings
just above back door

weight & weather could bring it
down at any moment but if not

door will eventually *strike*
and ice will kiss
concrete.

Nancy Julien Kopp lives and writes in the Flint Hills of Kansas. She has been published in various anthologies including 24 times in *Chicken Soup for the Soul* books, websites, newspapers, and magazines. She writes creative nonfiction, poetry, fiction for middle grade kids, and short memoirs. She shares writing knowledge through her blog which gives tips and encouragement to writers.

She blogs at www.writergrannysworld.blogspot.com

Ice Storm

Silver-coated trees on
a gray November day
lean ever lower,
reach out with icy fingers
to snag whatever lies
below.

Frigid beauty reigns,
frosted trees appear
lacy and delicate
despite the frozen
weight as they bow
to kiss the ground.

Norbert Góra is a 32 years old poet and writer from Poland. He is the author of more than 130 poems published in many poetry anthologies and magazines around the world. He also wrote three dark poetry books in English: *A Globe Bathed in Horror, Darkness in the End*, and *There Must be Something Between Dark and Light* (a collection of haikus) and one short story collection of horror, *Brutality*. He is inspired by both the light and the murkiness. Still looking for publishing opportunities in new languages.

Winter Reverie

Dance of snowflakes and wind
brings so much more with it,
memories swirl in front of my eyes,
it hurts to know how fast time flies.

Winter reverie continues,
icicles hang from the gutters,
the floe covers the lake like darkness,
a kiss of coolness on a December afternoon.

The last breath of this year is combined
with the sigh of the newborn heir,
winter, like a staple, holds the past
against the future, the coupler of the times.

Adriana Rocha was born in Bolivia. She is a psychologist. Poetry, photography, and educational psychology are her passions. Her journey into the world of words started in 2019. She has been participating in different literary events in Latin America, Spain, India, Canada, Nigeria, Australia, and the United States of America.

Winter Cure

I choose to be transformed
and I accept to be
taken by the wisdom
of nature,
please stay away
because
I got poison
On my lips
And the only
Cure is winter.

Irina Tall Novikova is an artist, graphic artist, and illustrator. She graduated from the State Academy of Slavic Cultures with a degree in art and also has a bachelor's degree in design. Her first personal exhibition *My soul is like a wild hawk* (2002) was held in the museum of Maxim Bagdanovich. In her works, she raises themes of ecology. In 2005, she devoted a series of works to the Chernobyl disaster and draws on anti-war topics. The first big series she drew was *The Red Book*, dedicated to rare and endangered species of animals and birds. She writes fairy tales and poems and illustrates short stories. She draws various fantastic creatures including unicorns, animals with human faces, and she especially likes the image of a man - a bird - Siren. In 2020, she took part in Poznań Art Week.

Follow her on:

https://instagram.com/irina369tall?igshid=YmMyMTA2M2Y=

https://m.facebook.com/profile.php?v=photos&lst=100009868569

https://www.instagram.com/irinanov4155/?hl=ru

The light of the fading day

lanterns are blazing with stars
Pedestrians as forgotten wanderers
seek in the warmth from the drops of cold autumn
I'll cry into the pillow, I'll kill longing with my hands
I'll make my heart stop
And the world died away, the thread ended ..

Swayam Prashant (pen-name of Dr. Prashanta Kumar Sahoo) was born in the undivided Cuttack district, Odisha. He was formerly an Associate Professor of English at Sarupathar College, Assam, India. He has written six books and two booklets: *Evaluation of Textbooks in the Teaching of English* (based on his Ph.D. thesis); *Values in Life* (based on a research project on Vedic and Upanishadic writings); *Knowledge Tree* (miscellaneous prose writings); *Haiku from the Garden of My Own* (poetry); *Live Like a Man* (poetry); *Premras Amrit* (poetry in Assamese); *Virgin Land Impregnated* (a thematic study of Canadian folk songs); and *Joy of Love* (a unique booklet of love poems).

Fiery Flakes

I dreamt that I was a ball of fire
whom they had chained in snow
but foolish as they were they didn't know
that however strong and cruel they might be
the snowy prison could never hold me
as long as I didn't allow myself to be.

I pretended to be powerless before them
by surrendering to their whips and blows.
In fact I was making myself strong enough
by turning my sinews into steel
but all my emotions were still soft
as soft as the petals of a rose.
I longed for my love in the clouds
I broke the snow hill into pieces
fiery flakes fell all over the earth
as I rose to the skies.

Alshaad Kara is a Mauritian poet who writes from his heart. His latest poems were published in one Magazine, *parABnormal Magazine September 2022* and three anthologies, *Les Gardeurs de Rêves*, *Love Letters to Poe, Volume 2: Houses of Usher*, and *20.35 Africa: An Anthology of Contemporary Poetry Vol. V.*

Wonders of the Night

Freezing coldness was spilled in the sky,
Making polar lights at night-time.

It was so wonderful,
Like a flickering curtain of pastel colours,

It was so enlightening,
Like magical threads spilled with pastel colours.

Was it the revenant of my dreams,
Or the revelation of this world,

Such minute details of this aurora,
Makes the night a lighting of enchanted wonders.

Where the Heart Met its Fall

The bridge of love, that's what I call it.
It was too beautiful to be realistic.

My heart was taken aback by this fall!

The snowfall made the Multnomah Falls,
A delight of romance on this earth.

I felt like I have fallen in another era of heaven.

My heart froze its love by looking at this beauty.

The leaves were like wings of snow,
The water was like the gates of heaven,

All was in alignment to make my heart fall,
At the Multnomah Falls,
During this snowfall.

Multnomah Falls in Winter Dress

Richard Oyama's poems, stories, and essays have appeared in *Premonitions: The Kaya Anthology of New Asian North American Poetry, The Nuyorasian Anthology, Breaking Silence, Dissident Song, A Gift of Tongues, About Place, Konch Magazine, Pirene's Fountain, Tribes, Malpais Review, Anak Sastra, Buddhist Poetry Review,* and other literary journals. *The Country They Know* (Neuma Books 2005) is his first collection of poetry. He has a Master of Arts in English: Creative Writing from San Francisco State University. Currently retired, Oyama taught at California College of Arts in Oakland, University of California at Berkeley, and University of New Mexico. His first novel in a trilogy, *A Riot Goin' On*, is forthcoming. He is currently at work on a young adult novel and a full-length poetry collection.

Winter Rain

Winter rain makes sodden a bed of leaves
On a hillside Eva scampers up in Joaquin
Miller Park, a feast of wet odors that

Excite her beyond sense. Walkers
Promise a view. Indeed
A vision opens of a green valley

And the flatlands below. Up here
Labyrinthine roots of live oak
Uncountable in anthropocene years

But not rings of antiquity. The rain
Subsides this spring afternoon.
At an elbow of the path

A small lake Eva and I skirt. Above
Cold water runnels down
Hill, silt and runoff, above

A veil of mist. In the scrim of fog
A shape above the fall:
My mother's wraith. Eva

And I quiet. We feel
A presence. It completes us.

Winter

Smoke of early dawn. Ocean clarity of thin air, lungs shocked. World made anew in morning light. Shadowy holes in rolling streets (white sheets crushed, unclean. Stigmata of acne). Snow gathers my knees, waves in a frozen sea. I sing no-songs to the silence. My old self, a withered ghost, passes. Shiver, bone rattle. None but imperfection, Death tells us: skeletal fracture, rent sinew. Ice freezes the palm at the end of the mind. Boughs shine above: a gift. Tangle of black branches glisten against the sun.

Ginger Zyskowski was raised in Kansas where she had a long career as a professional percussionist and music educator. In 2019, she retired to the Pacific Northwest where she enjoys writing and working with fibers. She has published two poetry chapbooks, *Love and Lovers* (2019), and *Another Think Coming! Poems and Stuff* (2020).

Art projects and book samples can be seen on her website - https://gingerz.works/

White

White -   as you bring with you that cold,
           beautiful softness of a first
           winter snow:

           Is it really only beauty you bring?

           As I share laughter and tears with my
           best friend, I notice you … floating,
           like underwater tendrils with a constant
           but gentle movement, at her temples.

           You tease me, as you peek out from the
           chests and bearded faces of men I love.
           "Here I come, ready or not!"
           Is that your game?

           More and more often you seem to snicker
           at me from here and there …
           and I am reminded.

           The watching of it doesn't get any easier.

           It is my hope that as you and I become
           closer, you allow me to meet you
           little by little,
           with a few close friends to share
           the watching.

Gitanjli Mridul is a poet and teacher from India. She earned a Masters' degree in English Language and Literature. She is a hilly woman from the beautiful hills of the Himalayas and writes in her native language of Hindi as well as English. She is a nature-loving poet.

Winter's Wonders

A thin sheet of mist
Enveloped me
And the morning sheen
As I'm on my walk
Of daily routine
Slight shiver and cool breeze
Caressing the flying curls
The world is yawning
Beneath silent dirt road
Hidden hibernating lives
Love lazy lizard lying
Permeating slumber
Rose petals shun dewy
Sluggishly licking lips of
Rays sentries
And still sleeping the sovereign sun
Under the thin sheet of mist
Shirker of duty
Winter's wonders relishing!

Victoria Puckering lives in Yorkshire, England and goes by the poetic name of Toria and the Naked Poet. Her work has been described as naked and raw. She writes original poetry of all genres and has only been writing for nearly four years. Her poems have been podcasted in New York, USA, on Drystone radio in Yorkshire, England, and on various poetry sites on Facebook.

This year, she became a published Poetess with her poetry appearing in following anthologies: *The Poppy: A Symbol of Remembrance* (Southern Arizona Press), the Dark Poetry Society anthologies, and Wheelsong Poetry.

Winter is Wide Awake

Winter is wide awake
Cold snowflake's fall
On the hard, frosted ground
The sun gleams
On the frozen blue lake
People skate in their warm coats with woolly scarves
    and brightly coloured mittens
The bare trees just glisten
As if, jewels laden their bare branches
Emerald green and ruby red
We sit beside a burning fire before bed
Warming up
After being out in the winter cold
The blackest sky
A silver moon
The sparkling stars
Tired from this cold day
Winter is here to stay
For several months until Spring makes its own way

My Own Snow Globe

Sitting in my comfy seat
As I look through the wooden window
Thick snowflakes fall
No human footsteps on the crisp white snow
Only cat's paws prints
Disturb the crunchy snowfall
The green grass covered in this glistening snow
I feel like I am in a snow globe
As I look through this unusual large window
The thick white sky with plenty of snowflakes on
    supply
The snowflake shaker way up high
Is spreading each unique snowflake far and wide
The dark leafless tree covered in white glistening ice
This winter picture brings such delights
As I sit in my comfy warm chair
Watching the natural snow globe outside
Glistening whiteness everywhere
No human footsteps in the snow
Only cat's paws prints
Disturb the crunchy snow
I'm sitting in my own snow globe

Pauline Thiele started writing poetry about 13 years ago. It all began with a phone call, when her family was told that their unborn child would not live. Consequently, he (Liam) was my very first inspiration. Almost all my poetry is rhyming, usually in a quatrain. Although I sometimes like to try different forms, particularly the French rondeau and an octave. But my greatest love is my family (husband, son, and daughter).

Hear the Winter Talk

Hear the winter talk, a language of her own,
Where only peace and love are known.
Watch her create a snowy flurry,
(Declaring all should slow down, not hurry)
and cold within the wind is blown.

Amongst the trees you'll hear her moan,
as she soaks the ground and new life is grown.
To the exhausted she gives mercy,
    hear the winter talk.

Where nature nurtures the new seeds sown,
the beauty of springs flowers are shown.
With temperatures that will vary,
she offers relief to the weary;
as a loving queen upon a throne,
    hear the winter talk.

Winter Morning
Ivan Choultse

Tasneem Hossain is a Bangladeshi multi-lingual poet. Her wanderings in other areas of literature include fiction, translation, academic pieces, columns, and op-eds. She writes in English, Bangla, and Urdu. Her writings appear in magazines, different dailies, and annual publications of different countries. To name a few: *International Human Rights Art Festival 2022 Anthology: Tyranny Unchained; Woman's Freedom, Borderless Journal* (Singapore), *Discover Mississauga and More - eBook* (Canada), *Krishnochura* (United Kingdom), *EDAS Chronicle, The Dhaka Literature, An Ekushey Anthology, The Daily Star, bdnews24.com,* and *Asian Age Online* (Bangladesh).

Her publications consist of *The Pearl Necklace* and *Floating Feathers (poetry),* and *Split and Splice (article).*

Three more of her publications will be available in a couple of months.

She runs a project named *Life in Verses* where she conducts poetry writing workshops.

She completed her Masters in English Language and Literature in 1986 from Dhaka University.

She is the Director of Continuing Education Centre (human capacity development organization). As a training consultant her expertise lies in Communication Management and Language. She worked as faculty (English Language) in Chittagong University of Engineering and Technology. She also worked as newscaster, commentary reader, and radio jockey in radio Bangladesh for 10 years. She directed Shakespeare's play *A Midsummer Night's Dream.*

She resides, sharing time, between Bangladesh and Canada.

Ice and Snow

Shining, sparkling snow and ice,
Fluffy flurries falling from heaven, oh so nice!
Hanging icicles on branches and leaves sparkle
      bright,
Brown black branches dressed in snow look so soft
      and white.
Sizzling sunrays on rooftops dazzle my eyesight.

Far away the snowcapped mountains and clouds
      above in the sky,
Glistening water of slippery ice makes me gasp and
      sigh;
Children's laughter making snowman, whistles past
      by.
Thick white cold feathers make my lips chapped dry;
Holiday makers with skates and skis rush swiftly to
      mountains high.

Tread on the soft velvety white snow very quiet,
Footsteps slow on the black ice, guess I have to be
      right,
Lest I fall and injure my waist or spine.
Trying not to get icy cold wind frostbites,
Hold on to my woolen clothes very tight.

Sipping hot coffee in front of the fireplace in a shawl,
Night is early, yet not dimming the world at all.
Glimmering moonlight on white jewels fall,
Brightening mother earth with such a pretty sight!
I sing and dance to celebrate in delight.

As the cold winter bids farewell and melts away the
    snow,
Beautiful delicate pink cherry blossoms grow.
Pink petals floating down carpeting the ground
    below;
Time to clean the garden and start to mow,
Daisies, daffodils, tulips and lilies, cherries, grapes
    and tangerines to sow;
Bask in the scent of spring and colors, to bloom and
    glow.

Deep inside, I yearn for more downy flakes.
Dazzling, dancing white angels from heaven;
I long for the magical white fairyland once again.
Alluring beauty of ice and snow cleanses my soul
    and sense.
Oh white fairy, please keep falling for wishful
    romance!

Colleen Moyne is a South Australian based writer, currently living and travelling full-time in a van with her greyhound, Winter.

Since completing studies in Professional Writing in 2013, Colleen has had poems and stories published in over thirty different collections, both in Australia and overseas. Her work has appeared as part of an audio book for the Fringe Festival and as radio plays for both the *Tales to Terrify* podcast and *Creepy* podcast. Her first solo poetry collection, *Time Like Coins*, was published in December of 2018. Her second book, *Called to Coddiwomple*, is due for release in 2023. She has won awards for her poetry. In 2013, she received the Mindshare Australia 'Open Your Mind' Poetry Award and was shortlisted for the 2015, 2016, 2017 and 2018 awards. She was long-listed for the COTA Zestfest award and placed second in the Ken Vincent Poetry Award. Her first book, *Time Like Coins* was nominated for an Anne Elder Award. On top of all this, she has established several writers' groups and teaches courses and workshops in all aspects of creative writing.

You can learn more about Colleen at:

www.colleenmoyne.com

Southern Arizona Press

I Called You Winter

The first day I saw you, I knew
that we were meant to meet.

A so-called 'reject'
from the greyhound track,
your timid auburn eyes melted into mine
and your long and clumsy legs
stepped into my heart.

I called you Winter,
not for the bleak, greyness
of the concrete and wire cage
that once was your home,

but for the ever-changing colours
of the winter sky,
for the newness
of a lush, green landscape,
freshly washed and ready
for the blossoming of spring.

For the joyful feeling
of soft blankets,
and the warmth
of a crackling wood fire
on a crisp night.

This is why I called you Winter.
This is what your life will now be -

New and fresh
and ready to blossom,
to feel the joy of soft blankets,
the warmth
of a crackling wood fire on a crisp night...
and all the love you deserve.

Van Life

Van life
brings the seasons home
more than a house
ever did before

The seasons
dictate how I live,
where I go
and what I explore.

Summer
is but to tolerate
to hibernate each day
under shady trees

But Winter
is to celebrate
to participate
and savor the crisp, biting breeze

To drink in the sight
of lush green hills,
flowing creeks,
and skies of blue and grey

To light a fire
and be soothed
by its crackling song
as the flames dance and sway

Then to sleep
curled in contentment,
rocked gently by the wind
and the lullaby of rain

And to wake
to a mist clothed landscape
defrosting in the morning sun
till all is green again.

Tim Kahl is the author of five books of poems, most recently *Omnishamble* (Bald Trickster, 2019) and *California Sijo* (Bald Trickster, 2022). He is also an editor of *Clade Song* [http://www.cladesong.com]. He builds flutes, plays them and plays guitars, ukuleles, charangos, and cavaquinhos as well. He currently teaches at California State University, Sacramento, where he sings lieder while walking on campus between classes.

Follow him at:

http://www.timkahl.com

https://soundcloud.com/tnklbnny

The Winter Cringe

The pores tighten during the advance of the clouds,
and the neck is taut edging past the crispness.
It is time to don the heavy socks and ponder
why the tule fog has gone missing the last
decade. It used to cripple traffic on the interstate,
create pileups that would make the headlines.
Now it's like an old man you hardly see
anymore without his walker. It's still the town
crier for winter, but it doesn't sock in the city's
air traffic like it used to. It has become an ache
in the bones that no one's sad to see leave.
Questions linger about the houses built on
the marshlands where the Miwok villages grew,
villages limited in size to avoid damage to the land.
The Miwok kept moving, some say all the way from
Siberia where much of their language still
plays. Who could blame them for getting
out of all that snow, following the salmon
across the Bering Strait and taking up residence
among the valley oaks. They built *kotça* houses
of bark and reeds, slept on furs. They
waited not for the bringer of fire,
but the bringer of socks. I am tired
of cringing and tensing up for the cold
coming this season. O coyote, great creator
of the Miwok, grant me anti-freeze in
the heart and toes that won't turn to ice.

Paul Gilliland retired after over 30 years of service with the US Army and settled in the high desert of Southeast Arizona, just miles from the historic wild west towns of Tombstone and Bisbee. He holds Associate of Applied Science Degrees in Intelligence Studies, Linguistics, and Education from Cochise College; a Bachelor of Arts Degree in Music Theory/Composition and Technical Theater Design from Olivet College; and a Master of Fine Arts Degree in Music Composition from the Vermont College of Fine Arts. He is an educator, composer of 21st century chamber music, author, form poet, and publisher. He is a member of the American Society of Composers, Authors, and Publishers (ASCAP); National Writers Union; Authors Guild; Poetry Society of America; the Academy of American Poets; and the Association for Publishers for Special Sales. In addition to teaching interviewing techniques and report writing for the US Army, he is the Editor-in-Chief of his own publishing company, Southern Arizona Press. He currently has two published volumes of poetry, *Hindsights of 2020* and *The Journey of the Fool: A Poetic Journey in Three Parts*, both available through Amazon. His third book of verse, *A Heroic Crown and Other Sonnets* is set to be released at the end of 2022 and he is currently working on completing his fourth collection of poetry, *Tales from a Southwest Inn*. His poetry appears online in numerous Facebook poetry group as well as being published in *Sonnet Sanctuary Anthology Volume 1* (A Romeo Nation), *Open Skies Quarterly Volumes 4, 5, 6, Perceptions, Dark Reflections*, and *Myths, Legends, and Lore* (Shrouded Eye Press), and *From Sunset to Sunrise* (Dark Poetry Society Anthology).

He can be followed online at:

https://www.facebook.com/PaulGillilandPoetry
https://www.facebook.com/SouthernArizonaPress
http://www.PaulGillilandMusic.com/
https://www.SouthernArizonaPress.com/

On a Cold and Brisk December Night
(Pantoum)

On a cold and brisk December night
The cloudless sky's a pallet of
The full moon high and glowing bright
And twinkling stars that shine above.

The cloudless sky's a pallet of
The moonlight's luminescent glow
And twinkling stars that shine above
The newly fallen winter snow.

The moonlight's luminescent glow
Upon the frozen forest floor
Where newly fallen winter snow
Provides the setting as before.

Upon the frozen forest floor
The full moon high and glowing bright
Provides the setting as before
On a cold and brisk December night.

The Winter Wind
(Long Form Fibonacci Poem)

The winter wind blows all around

As cold and frosty snow doth fall

It leaves a blanket on the ground
That covers over gardens all

The frozen breath with chilling sound
Provides the icy winter's call
That drives all people homeward bound

Inside the cabin warm and dry
We gather round the blazing log
Upon the couches soft we lie
To cuddle with our faithful dog
A loyal aging Basset Hound

The setting sun and evening gloam
Will usher in the winter night
While we are snuggled safe at home
The winter moon is shining bright
It gives a luster to the snow
That blankets every glen and field
And in the village down below
It drifts where fencerows fail to yield

And near the stream and frozen bog
The snowy owl sounds its cry
As it takes flight amidst the fog
For unexpected prey to spy
Beyond the distant garden wall

Within the limbs of timbers tall
Is where the snowy flakes are found
For here is where they cease to fall

The snow that slowly blankets all
And covers every spot of ground

As each flake softly starts to fall

The winter wind blows them around

Desert Winter Nights

The full wolf moon is nearing
And coldness starts to fall
As clouds of night start clearing
The owl sounds her call

The north wind blows with ire
And flakes of snow appear
The air starts getting drier
This first month of the year

For every desert creature
Must now get out of sight
As they hide every feature
Beneath the ground of white

Below the full moon shimmer
The owl in stealthy flight
Glides quiet in the glimmer
Of this cold winter night

As creatures leave their covers
To find a tiny meal
The owl in silent hovers
Their fate to quickly seal

The stillness of the gloaming
Is broke by the attack
As animals still roaming
All quickly scamper back

Retreating into burrows
They find a brief reprise
From windblown snow that whirls
To mask the owl's surprise

The wolf moon gives a luster
On flakes reflecting light
Amidst the winter bluster
On this cold desert night

215

Jack Frost's Nightly Art
(Sonnet)

The briskness of a January morn
When rays of sun are slow to break the day
Reveal the frosted windows that were born
Throughout the night when Jack was left to play.
Each morning's breath is filled with air so clean;
Invigorating life among the old.
The glow of embers lingering between
The frosted glass of nighttime's winter cold.
For as the sun begins to warm the air
And temperatures outside begin to rise,
Our dear friend Jack retires in the glare
Of light infused throughout his frosted guise.
We stay to watch the breaking of the dawn
Until the art of Jack is all but gone.

On a Cold Winter's Night

A flurry of flakes
In the winter of white
Like the twinkling stars
On a cold winter's night

The whirling of winds
Send flakes all a flutter
Freezing icicles
That hang from the gutter

We stare through the pane
At the frosty delight
Trapped in a snow globe
On a cold winter's night

The Rapture of the Newly Fallen Snow
(Sonnet)

The quarter moon shines down without a sound
As downy flakes of snow begin to fall
To form a pure white blanket on the ground
A peacefulness of which I can't recall
The moon shine gives a luster to the chaste
And pureness of the untouched virgin white
Creating magic scenes all inter-laced
Translucent in the ever-changing night
But as the wind blows swiftly 'cross the fields
And drives the snow to drift along the trees
It proves the strength and power that it yields
To do with virgin flakes how e'er it please
The rapture of the newly fallen snow
Below the twinkling stars and soft moon glow

The Wonders of Winter

Meet the Selection Editor

Timothy Couchman served in the US Army and left military service in 2020. He obtained a bachelor's degree in Music History and Literature in 2002. He currently lives in Southeast Arizona.

We are very pleased to have Timothy join the Southern Arizona Press team and take on the daunting task of reading and selecting the poems for inclusion in this anthology. His work is greatly appreciated.

The previous 2022 anthologies from Southern Arizona Press

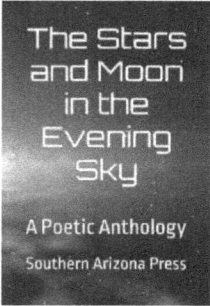

The Stars and Moon in the Evening Sky

is a collection of 120 poetic works crafted by 65 poets from across the globe inspired by the universe around us.

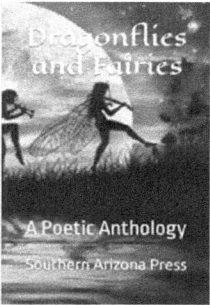

Dragonflies and Fairies

is a collection of 72 poetic works crafted by 34 poets from across the globe celebrating the magical and mystical creatures of folklore.

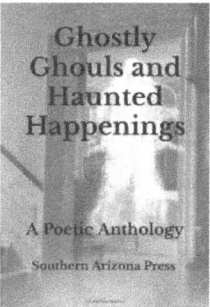

Ghostly Ghouls and Haunted Happenings

is a collection of 129 poetic works crafted by 46 poets from across the globe inspired by ghosts, ghouls, and things that go bump in the night.

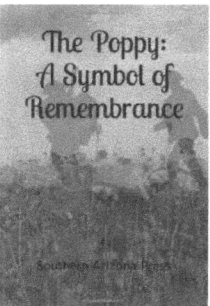

The Poppy: A Symbol of Remembrance

examines the history of the poppy as a flower of remembrance, the story of Colonel John McCrae and his poem "In Flanders Fields", and the work of the "Poppy Ladies" Moina Michael and Madame Anna Guerin and how they influenced the adoption of the poppy as a memorial flower of remembrance. The volume includes 20 Answer or Response poems to McCrae's Poem written between 1918 and 1925, 21 lyrics from songs about Flanders and the Poppy written between 1918 and 1924, 38 poems of remembrance written by World War One poets between 1912 and 1921, and 79 poems written by 21st Century poets from around the globe in remembrance of the fallen heroes from all war of the last century.

The upcoming 2023 anthologies from Southern Arizona Press

Love Letters in Poetic Verse – A collection of romantic poetic works for Valentine's Days. Coming in early February 2023.

Castles and Courtyards – An anthology from 21st Century poetic bards celebrating the medieval life of kings, courts, peasants, and troubadours. Coming in early April 2023.

A Midsummer Night's Dream – An anthology of poems celebrating the plot lines of Shakespeare's famous comedy: Weddings, the Woodland, the Realm of Fairyland, Under the Light of the Moon, along with poems about the summer solstice (Litha) and any other fond memories of summers past. Coming in early June 2023.

Beyond the Sand and Sea – A gathering of poetic works inspired by the sea, seashore, lighthouses, or anything else associated with life on or near the sea. Coming in early August 2023.

The Children's Book of Bedtime Verse – A collection of poetic works appropriate for reading to children at bedtime. Coming in early October 2023.

Home for the Holidays – A holiday anthology of poetic works celebrating the gathering of family during the fall and winter holidays. Coming in early December 2023.

Poets interested in submitting works for upcoming anthologies are asked to check out our Current Submissions page at: http://www.southernarizonapress.com/current-submissions/ for more information about each anthology and our process for submission.

Published works by our featured contributors

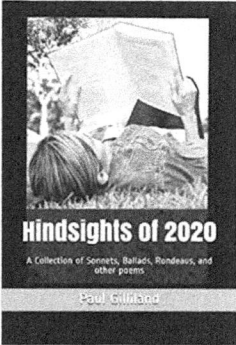

Paul Gilliland's **Hindsights of 2020** is a collection of 69 poems written during the last five months of 2020. It includes sonnets, ballads, rondeaus, and other poems influenced by patriotism, love of nature and astrology, and reflections on memories and the world we live in.

https://www.amazon.com/dp/B08STHXXGT

Paul Gilliland's **The Journey of the Fool** is a poetic journey in three parts: Part 1 – *The Journey of the Fool* - A poetic journey through the 22 cards of the Major Arcana Tarot deck each written in a different poetic form. Part 2 – *The Zodiac Sonnets* – A collection of 25 Shakespearean sonnets about each of the Tropical and Chinese Zodiac Signs. Part 3 – *Full Moons and Druid Sabbats* – A collection of 45 poems depicting each of the full moons, Druid Sabbats, holidays, and other astronomical events presented in chronological order.

https://www.amazon.com/dp/B09PMH12BW

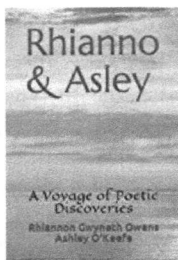

Rhiannon Owens and Ashley O'Keefe join forces as Rhianno & Asley to take readers on voyages of poetic discoveries in the series of poetic collections:

A Voyage of Poetic Discoveries

https://www.amazon.com/Rhianno-Asley-Voyage-Discoveries-Collections/dp/B08B325GPT

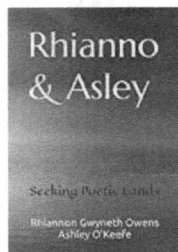

Seeking Poetic Lands

https://www.amazon.com/Rhianno-Asley-Seeking-Poetic-Lands/dp/B08L7W5PWJ

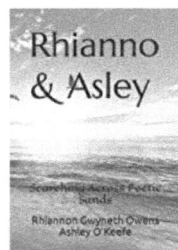

Searching Across Poetic Sands

https://www.amazon.com/Rhianno-Asley-Searching-Across-Poetic/dp/B098GJDCTP

In Poetic Dreams

https://www.amazon.com/Rhianno-Asley-Poetic-Ashley-OKeefe/dp/B09SNW7G69

Nocturnals

https://www.amazon.com/Rhianno-Asley-Nocturnals-Ashley-OKeefe/dp/B0B5KQSKVN

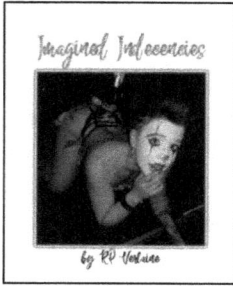

Imagined Indecencies is Rp Verlaine's third book. Poetry that is Profusely Illustrated with color photos taken by Verlaine of models and friends who posed for him. The poems are haiku, Seneru, sonnets, and one-line poems. A notable change from previous books is there are several free verse poems as well. All the poems have been published before in Literary Journals, Magazines, Newspapers, and websites. They have been published in Japan, Africa, Wales, Scotland and of course Verlaine's native America.

https://www.amazon.com/Imagined-Indecencies-Rp-Verlaine/dp/145663867X

In **Time Like Coins**, Colleen Moyne looks at the 'ordinary' things in life and makes them extraordinary with her gentle, nuanced observations, where frost becomes toffee, and dew drops become thousands of miniature rainbows. Colleen sees things and thinks deeply about them. Whether finding solace after loss, in the lives of tiny ducklings, or examining herself gently and honestly, via the face she sees in her own mirror, Colleen's words will strike chords with our lives, as she shows us glimpses into her own examined life. – Carolyn Cordon

https://www.amazon.com/Time-Like-Coins-Colleen-Moyne/dp/176041669X

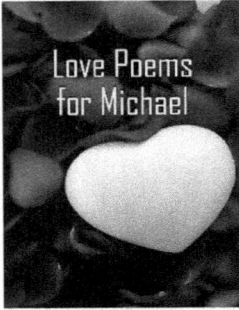

Love Poems for Michael by Joan McNerney Many reflect on New England with autumn foliage and fierce winters. However, four seasons do include bursting springs and boiling summers. Love is its own season, its own country, its own domain. Let's explore love up north during spring and summer.

https://www.amazon.com/Love-Poems-Michael-Joan-McNerney/dp/9388319656

https://www.cyberwit.net/publications/1602

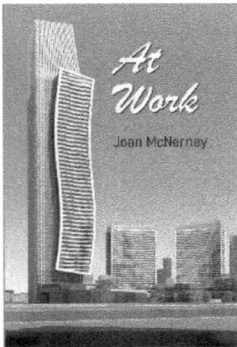

At Work by Joan McNerney explores everyday workers. It is unique because each worker, either female or male, receives their own page. These are snapshots of people who are either content with or made unhappy by their daily circumstances. Reading this book is an exploration of human nature at its core.

https://www.amazon.com/At-Work-Joan-McNerney/dp/8182537835

https://www.cyberwit.net/publications/1759

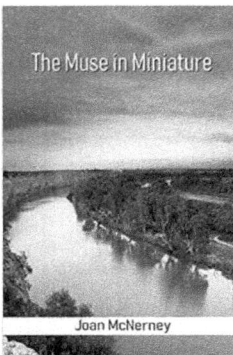

The Muse in Miniature by Joan McNerney There is no doubt this poet very aptly traverses an immense range of emotion and experience. Here we find poetry's passion and powerful imagination in rich abundance.

https://www.amazon.com/Muse-Miniature-Joan-McNerney/dp/9389074509

https://www.cyberwit.net/publications/1262

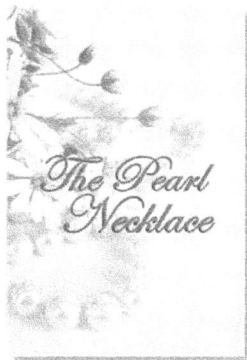

Poetry to Tasneem Hossain is an ever-flowing river reflecting all that surrounds us. **The Pearl Necklace** is a lyrical journey of sensitivity and contemplation through life in its different colors and shades. The title poem is about unfulfilled true love. *The Invisible Cord* is a celebration of mother's love. *Agony* is a cry for social justice. The last poem *The Lighthouse* ends with an aspiration to make our existence more meaningful. The essence of her poems is the beauty of nature and human life.

https://forms.gle/4JdcJi792ZSZS63R7

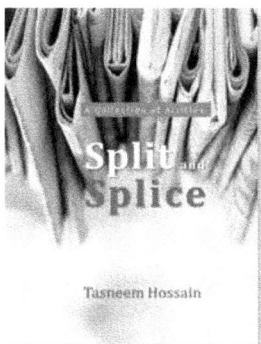

The poems of Tasneem Hossain's **Floating Feathers** are an outcome of the spiraling moments of her emotional outbursts. The title poem is a confession of the poetic thoughts floating and falling into her lap. *Let's Walk Together, You and I* deals with old age agonies and pains of becoming senile. Human emotions, social justice, kindness towards humanity and transience of life are some of the themes of her poetry. At the end there is a collection of haiku poems.

https://forms.gle/4JdcJi792ZSZS63R7

Tasneem Hossain's book **Split and Splice** is a compilation of some of the writer's articles published in different newspapers dealing with historical events and interesting facts about different issues, some are about acquiring good habits for a peaceful and successful life, some discuss ways of improving lifestyles and overall well-being having relevance to day to day life. The different aspects of life will help readers to become more conscious of life and the world surrounding them.

https://forms.gle/4JdcJi792ZSZS63R7

D.C. Buschmann's first poetry collection, **Nature: Human & Otherwise** is a selection of poems that highlight the human condition, good and bad, and present them alongside what animals do instinctively as part of their nature.

https://www.amazon.com/Nature-Human-Otherwise-D-C-Buschmann/dp/B08W7MWVC5

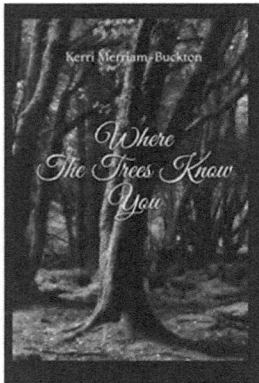

Kerri Merriam-Buckton's **Where the Trees Know You** is a love story that opens with Rowan grappling with her new identity as a single woman, after her husband's affair and their subsequent separation and wondering how to move forward. When a message from the past thought to be long gone returns to her, this, along with her family's urging, convinces her to get away from it all and travel back to Ireland, a land she has always felt drawn to, and a place she remembers being truly happy. But this trip will become more than something to lift Rowan's spirits. It will teach her lessons in love, forgiveness, saving oneself, and the true meaning of home.

https://www.amazon.ca/Where-Trees-Know-Kerri-Merriam-Buckton/dp/B08CM89MJT

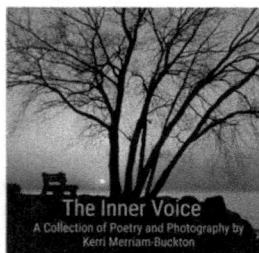

Kerri Merriam-Buckton's **The Inner Voice,** is a collection of poetry on various subject matters with coinciding photography to accompany them.

https://www.amazon.ca/Inner-Voice-Collection-Photography-Merriam-Buckton/dp/B09HR6HVVF

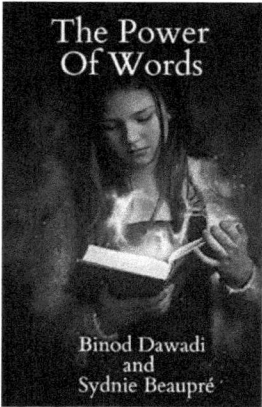

Poetry is magic, weaving tapestries via lilting words, creating a stunning visual of the author's ideas. **The Power Of Words** is the debut poetry collection of author Binod Dawadi, edited by bestselling author Sydnie Beaupré.

https://www.amazon.com/dp/B0B3L6VLGG

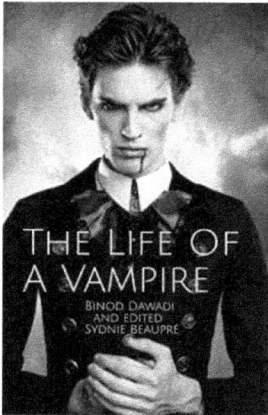

Binod Dawadi's **The Life of a Vampire** follows Binod, who was not a bad vampire, he worked helping people and doing good things. The vampire kingpin heard of this and sicced evil vampires on him, forcing him to do terrible deeds. He refused because he is a true hero. Go on Binod's journey as he tries to find a woman as good as him, and as he tries to combat evil at every cost.

https://www.amazon.com/dp/B0B3GNQQFT

The Power of Words 2 is Binod Dawadi's sequel to the **The Power of Words**. A collection of poems and short stories about love, hate, happiness, sadness, wars, etc. to motivate people and make them aware of such things in life. The 26 letters of the alphabet are the twenty-six voices of God coming to earth to serve people in modern times.

https://www.amazon.com/Power-Words-2-Binod-Dawadi-ebook/dp/B0BB68KYW7

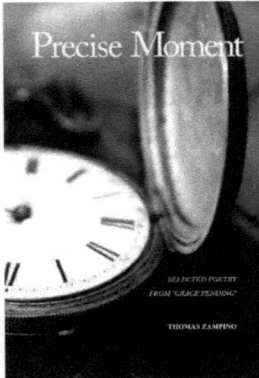

After nearly 40 years as a corporate and property tax attorney in NYC, Thomas Zampino's poems just about popped into existence at the *Precise Moment* when they could no longer be held back. This is a broad selection of mostly simple observations about life, faith, and meaning as seen through the eyes of someone who was profoundly touched by the world around him long before he realized it. Influenced by American poet Billy Collins and English poet David Whyte, these poems are a reflection of the aging - and hopefully the maturing - process in real time.

https://www.blurb.com/b/10812828-precise-moment-pb

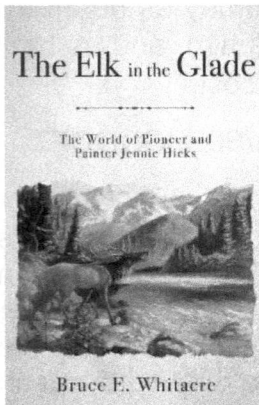

Publishers Weekly BookLife Editors Pick: Based on personal memories and family oral history, *The Elk in the Glade: The World of Pioneer and Painter Jennie Hicks*, Bruce E. Whitacre's debut collection of sixteen poems traces the life and legacy of a family matriarch, his great grandmother, Jennie Hicks. The daughter of American pioneers, she marries a successful farmer, bearing him three girls, seeing them all married, only to outlive him and the farm. Once again alone and facing hardship, she transforms an almost forgotten hobby, her young girl dream, into a brilliant thirty-year career as a successful landscape painter, the future pride of her hometown, Farnam, Nebraska, and an important figure in American art. Lovers of American history, art, and strong female characters will enjoy these lyric chronicles.

https://www.amazon.com/Elk-Glade-Pioneer-Painter-Jennie/dp/1946116254

Late Snows and other Selected Facebook Poems: A Walk Along the North Main Street is a collection of John Anthony Fingleton poems mainly taken from my Facebook postings over the years and other scattered anthologies. The poems in this volume are in no chronological order, except the final poem section which represents my Norse/Viking writings.

https://www.amazon.com/Snows-other-Selected-Facebook-Poems/dp/B0BJYD45PV

Marianne Tefft's poetry collection is inspired by the phases of the Moon - waxing, full, waning, and new – **Full Moon Fire** traces the journey of love from bright to bittersweet and back again. Born under the Caribbean sky, these 40 "spoken songs" are romantic poems that speak to every heart that has ever loved under the full Moon.

https://www.amazon.com/Full-Moon-Fire-Spoken-Songs/dp/0228876451

www.ingramcontent.com/pod-product-compliance
Lightning Source LLC
Chambersburg PA
CBHW060740050426
42449CB00008B/1278